Finding the Missing Something

Living On Purpose for God's Purpose

Mary Graziano Scro

Finding the Missing Something: *Living On Purpose for* God's *Purpose*

Copyright © 2022 by Mary Graziano Scro

All rights reserved.

No part of this publication may be reproduced, stored in a retrieval system, or transmitted in any form or by any means, electronic, photocopying, recording, or otherwise, without the prior permission of the copyright holder.

Unless otherwise noted, Scriptures are taken from the Holy Bible, New International Version®, NIV®. Copyright © 2011 by Biblica, Inc.™ All rights reserved worldwide.

Scriptures referenced with (NLT) are taken from the Holy Bible, New Living Translation, copyright © 1996, 2004, 2007, 2013, 2015 by Tyndale House Foundation. All rights reserved.

Scriptures referenced with (MSG) are taken from The Message Bible, © 1993, 1994, 1995, 1996, 2000, 2001, 2002.

Scriptures referenced with (AMPC) are taken from The Amplified Bible, Old Testament, © 1965 and 1987 by The Zondervan Corporation, and from The Amplified New Testament, © 1954, 1958, 1987 by The Lockman Foundation.

Scriptures referenced with (NKJV) are taken from the New King James Version, © 1979, 1980, 1982 by Thomas Nelson, Inc., Publishers.

Cover design by Hannah Linder Creations LLC

Author's website: www.MaryGScro.com
LinkedIn: https://www.linkedin.com/in/mary-scro-0916/
Facebook: https://www.facebook.com/marygscro

*To my mentor, friend, and former pastor
Joe Sarver,
who went home to Jesus in 2004.*

*The first day I walked into Joe's church,
the Lord said,
This is my man, Joe. Sit under him and learn.*

I did.

Contents

Why Are We Here?	9
THE BEGINNING	15
1. My Salvation Testimony	17
2. Become a Disciple of Jesus	24
PLANNING	33
3. Recognize Your Responsibility	35
4. Determine Your Goal	39
5. Resolve to Act	43
BASIC TRAINING	49
6. Read the Bible	51
7. Repent From Your Sins	59
8. Forgive as God Forgives You	73
LIFESTYLE	81
9. Grow in Intimacy with God	83
10. Exchange the World's Ways for God's Ways	87
11. Share Your Testimonies	106
Why We Are Here	129
Endnotes	134

Why Are We Here?

Have you repeatedly tried to fill the void inside, but yet remain empty? Do you find yourself on a treadmill of trying one thing after another, but nothing lasts? Do you think about the meaning of not just your life, but of life overall?

Me too, for a long time! On the surface, it appeared I had everything. I loved my job and enjoyed a successful career in Information Technology. I had a loving family and loyal friends. I was not married at the time (two prior marriages ended in divorce), but these days marriage doesn't equate to success; I was happy in my single life.

Yet, I felt empty. I had an emptiness inside that remained no matter how good life appeared on the outside. I even searched out spiritual things in general because it seemed there had to be something more to life than what I could see.

But it all fell flat. The unsettling emptiness remained.

And then, through a series of circumstances that I can see in hindsight were totally God-arranged, Jesus found me and I gave my life to Him (details in Chapter 1, My Salvation Testimony).

I realized that it was not *something* missing from my life, but *Someone*! Inviting Jesus into my heart filled the emptiness; making Jesus Lord over my life and living for Him every day has given my life meaning and purpose. We are eternal beings, created by a loving Father God to live with Him forever. All the earthly things we enjoy are but a blip in the span of eternity. Only people live forever.

That's not me, you might be thinking. Perhaps you go to church every Sunday but still feel empty. Or, maybe you have a spiritual life, in general, and believe there is a God out there somewhere. Maybe you even pray to God in times of trouble and He answers. I did all of those at one point; but only when I entered a true relationship with Jesus and made an effort to grow my faith did the emptiness leave for good.

Here are three important lessons I learned about the process of growing in faith:

1. We must sometimes unlearn before we can learn.

Since I dedicated my life to Jesus at 35, I had to unlearn many behaviors from living in a very ungodly world and then re-learn God's ways. Many of the world's ways are centered on us and what we can do to be happy here on earth. God's way is the way of love and is based upon what we can do for others that will lead to them knowing Jesus. Each day, I can choose to invest time knowing God more by reading His Word and spending time with Him or do what I feel like doing and plop myself in front of the TV. I can choose to accept and be thankful for what I have and focus on what I can give to others, or complain about what God hasn't done yet for me or how life is unfair. I can choose to obey something God has clearly told me to do or choose to do what I want instead.

2. We exchange things in our life, not give up or lose them.

Everything in life has a price. Buying an item at the store costs money; and if you don't pay the price, the cost is you don't get the item. Losing weight and gaining health cost time and discipline; but if you don't do it, the cost is you continue to feel lousy, clothes don't fit, you take on health risks, and so on.

The same is true for spiritual peace. The cost of clinging to your old ways—with your focus on the earthly life—is that you'll never discover the peace, joy, and fullness of life that only God can provide. If you are willing to pay the price to give up the old ways and live with eternal focus, you gain God's increased peace and joy.

The goal is to surrender everything—all you are and all you have—so you fill up with more of God's life. More about that as you read.

3. Everyone has the opportunity to choose Jesus.

As human beings, we are alike in three fundamental ways. First, we all have breath—we're alive. Secondly, we all have 24 hours in a day, seven days a week, and 52 weeks in a year—the same amount of time no matter who we are. And third, we all have free will—the freedom to choose how we will spend that time, and thereby choose what we will build with our lives and who we will become. Therefore, we each have the opportunity to choose Jesus – God's grace is available to everyone who chooses it.

As you can see, a common thread in these lessons is choice. *You are the only one who can make your life what you want it to be.* The quality of your life is up to you – you are the master of your own destiny, so to speak. If you want things in your life to change, you need to choose to change them.

My hope through this book is to share some of what I've learned to encourage you that investing in a relationship with Jesus is hands down the best decision you will make *for eternity*. Like physical fitness, becoming spiritually fit takes a decision to change, setting goals, and discipline. Woven into this book are physical fitness analogies to help guide your journey. At the end of every chapter is a simple prayer to remind you that Jesus will help you every step of the way; you only need to ask.

Jesus died to make it possible for us to live as we were created to live: abundantly and to the fullest, as His children forever.

> The thief comes only in order to steal and kill and destroy. I came that they may have and enjoy

life, and have it in abundance (to the full, till it overflows).

— John 10:10 (AMPC)

Life to the full God gives us is about our entire being.

May God himself, the God of peace, sanctify you
through and through. May your whole spirit,
soul and body be kept blameless at the coming
of our Lord Jesus Christ.

— 1 Thessalonians 5:23

When we live fully for God, His love is revealed, and the Kingdom of God advances so that many will come to the saving knowledge of Jesus Christ and spend eternity in heaven with Him.

And *that* is what life is all about.

Will you say this prayer with me?

Dear Jesus,

Please reveal Yourself to me. I want to know the truth about You and about God the Father. I don't know what I need, but I know I need something more. Please help me find what I'm missing. Thank You!

In Your name I pray, Amen.

THE BEGINNING

MEET JESUS

Chapter 1
My Salvation Testimony
How God Won My Heart

My journey to sold-out faith in Jesus Christ was a somewhat long and analytical trip. Along the way, God spoke through His Word and through several key people who influenced both my decision to follow Jesus and my life as a Jesus follower once I made the decision. This is my testimony.

I was raised in a wonderful family—our parents loved us dearly and we all knew that. As Catholics, we attended mass every Sunday, CCD (Sunday school) classes, and participated in all the rituals along the way. The Bible verses and stories I read and heard laid a solid foundation for my knowledge of God but did very little to help me understand how to live in a relationship with God. I also didn't understand true salvation: salvation by faith in Christ where your identity is changed by the power of the Holy Spirit, and you enter a living, breathing, daily relationship with Jesus. I *performed* for God, but didn't relate to Him as my Father, or to Jesus as my Lord. And since I was taught that faith and religion were private matters, we seldom talked about our faith in or our relationship with God.

I am not condemning the Catholic faith in any way. I'm just relating my experience. I know many Catholics who have come to awesome saving faith in Jesus and have a wonderful relationship with Him. It just didn't happen that way for me.

Once I graduated from high school and moved out on my own, church attendance stopped except for the obligatory Easter and Christmas services. During the next 15 years, I married and divorced twice (with no children from either marriage), developed a successful career in Information Technology, and achieved a Bachelor's degree in Business Administration by attending night school. While I enjoyed my successful career, and my personal life moved along after my second divorce, I knew something was missing. I felt restless and empty, so I began searching for the proverbial "meaning of life."

In 1990, three significant events happened that guided my quest in a specific spiritual direction.

First, I met one of my cousins who lived differently because of a very solid faith in Jesus, yet hanging out with her was fun. Up until that time, I thought born-again disciples of Jesus were weird. Every time I ran into them, they were either smiling, pleasant, and sappy-happy or they were hypocritical, judgmental, and stern. I wanted no part of either kind. But my cousin and her friends were just down-to-earth, normal people like me; yet they had a peace I knew I didn't possess.

Next, my brother and sister-in-law bought me a Bible for my birthday, and that led me to consider going back to church again. I found a Catholic church nearby and started to attend, teaching 4th grade Sunday school and working in the nursery.

A third event that kept me on the path toward God happened the next year. I worked closely with another born-again disciple of Jesus on a consulting project. She too had a peaceful, rock-solid faith and was 100 percent certain of what she believed. She accepted me fully as I was, even with all my "warts" and flaws! I can remember talking about the leap of faith I felt I needed to take. We had more than a few conversations that went something like this:

Me: "What if it isn't true?"

Her: "But it is!"

Me: "What if I leap and it doesn't work?"

Her: "But it will!"

She never once wavered or doubted. I wanted that sense of security, but I had so many questions. Having the natural-born blessing/curse of an extremely active and analytical mind, I could not jump in without knowing for sure that it was true. I also had concerns about all I'd have to "give up" if I became a disciple of Jesus. Would life suddenly become boring? Would I never have any fun again?

God knows how to provide what we need instead of what we think we want. By then I was actively looking for someone who could answer all my questions so I could take a "leap of faith" with 100 percent certainty. I didn't understand at the time that the very word *faith* meant acting *in the midst of* what looks like uncertainty. Instead, God sent another strong and loving disciple of

Jesus to me who absolutely refused to engage in any debates of any kind.

I had changed churches and started attending a more Evangelical church very close to my house. My friend taught a class for new disciples of Jesus at that church. By God's divine design, I was the only one in the class so I had her undivided attention. I kept challenging her with question after question about Jesus and about Paul's letters. Her repeated, simple response (are you seeing a theme here?) was, "All God wants you to do is love Him and let Him love you." She said this to me over and over and over again.

At that time, I thought Jesus was an arrogant snob. He asserted that *He* was the way, *He* was the truth, *and He* was the only one. Who did He think He was, this Jesus? And Paul's letters had so many stern "do" and "do not" commands. All I saw was the Bible putting impossible behavioral goals in front of me, as dictated by this pompous Jesus and this hard-lined Paul. Then I had these women in my life who refused to defend Him or argue about His words; instead they peacefully and fully radiated His love toward me.

Although I felt myself softening, I could not get past all the questions in my logical and analytical mind. Then my loving Father God played His trump card, so to speak, almost two years after I received the Bible – the year of my 35th birthday.

My Salvation Testimony 21

I was traveling from a wedding in New Jersey back to my contract job in Iowa. Picture a huge wide-body jet, 2-5-2 seating, and only one-third full at the most. I was in a window seat, spread out for comfort with a good book, all my questions clamoring for attention. Someone had the nerve to sit next to me! I guess my look must have telegraphed my thoughts quite clearly because the man (I'll call him Rich) apologetically said, "I'll move when we get started, no problem."

Then he noticed a book I was reading – *Inside Out* by Larry Crabb. As he prepared to move, Rich looked at the book, cocked his head as though listening to someone, and then said, "Interesting book. Do you like it?" We talked a bit about it, and with that began the most amazing conversation I've ever had.

Rich was a strong, loving disciple of Jesus on his way home from a business trip. We talked the whole trip about the book, the Bible, Jesus, God, and other areas of faith, including many of my questions.

In itself, it was not an unusual conversation. We found no cure for cancer, the world's problems were left unsolved, and we did not delve into deep personal issues. What made it amazing was the delivery: Rich knew my questions, word for word, before I could ask them. As I was thinking of a question—for example, *How did they know Mary was a virgin?*— Rich would cock his head as though listening and say, "Did you ever wonder how they knew Mary was a virgin?" Then he'd proceed to either answer the question, or refer me to a verse or book that would help me discover the answer on my own.

This "mind-reading" dialogue went on for two solid

hours. After the first hour, I broke down in tears and shared with him what had been happening. Tears of gratitude formed in his eyes. He had indeed been listening to the Lord's still small voice (remember how he kept cocking his head to the side) and had been hesitant to speak because the questions seemed so random. But he knew the Lord's voice through years of obedience and dedication to spending time with Him, so he stepped out in faith and God spoke through him in the specific way I needed to hear. I got back to my hotel in Iowa, threw myself down on the bed, and committed the rest of my life to following the Lord: "God, You win!" My walk with Jesus began.

Jesus did not barge His way into my life. He wooed me and won my heart as only He could do. I received His gift of salvation by faith—not by earning it or by my performance. The moment I did, my eternal life with Him began.

Eight months later, I moved to Illinois and attended a church which had an awesome singles' group. I began to see that a completely different culture existed. And I quickly realized that while I had received my new life by faith, I had a responsibility to invest in my relationship with God if I wanted my faith to grow. My new friends lived what they believed – they were positive, kind, and intentional about their choices. We had lots of good, clean fun when we got together. I learned that you can have fun without drinking to get drunk and without being physically intimate.

Since then I've been blessed and disciplined. I've fallen down and I've been lifted up. I have been miraculously transformed and healed of many hurts and sins from the past. I received a precious gift from the Lord of the most wonderful husband, Don, at just the right time (more about him in later chapters). I've learned—many times through failure—that the more I obey and choose God's way, the faster and more deeply He can change me. How much He changes me is directly related to my peace, joy, and contentment in life.

More importantly, the more I'm changed the more loving I become with so much more to give to others. In fact, without being changed, I have nothing of value to give because I cannot give what I don't possess. While I know I've come a long way, I also realize I still have so much yet to learn and lots of growing to do…for as long as I am on this earth.

With the emptiness gone for good, I'm looking forward, not back, and moving closer to Jesus every day. I pray you have the desire to do the same.

Chapter 2
Become a Disciple of Jesus
Create Your Salvation Testimony

The first choice we all must make before we can enjoy a relationship with Jesus or grow in spiritual fitness is to become a disciple of Jesus. A disciple is someone who is a true follower of Jesus and not someone who claims to be a disciple because their family is "Christian" or they attend church.

I am purposely not using the word "Christian" because it is overused and watered down in our culture. Jesus called His followers disciples, and charged them to go make disciples.

> Therefore go and make disciples of all nations,
>   baptizing them in the name of the Father and of
>   the Son and of the Holy Spirit,
>
> — Matthew 28:19

If you know you *aren't* a disciple of Jesus or you're not sure, turn to the end of this chapter for scriptures that will help you understand what the Bible says about being a disciple. As Jesus, Paul, and John tell us in those scriptures, being a true disciple of Jesus requires us to:

1. Believe Jesus is Lord and that God raised Him from the dead.
2. Confess that you are a sinner and need Jesus.
3. Repent and change who is in charge of your life by turning from your own way and inviting Jesus to be Lord of your life.

When you read about Jesus's disciples in the gospels and Acts, the focus of their ministry is people's eternal destination. Yes, Jesus healed, and yes, Jesus provided food. But the main goal was not temporary relief, it was for people to see God's love for them. And it was to open the door for them to hear the truth about Jesus and their need for Him.

> Jesus answered, "I am the way and the truth and the life. No one comes to the Father except through me."
>
> — John 14:6

> for all have sinned and fall short of the glory of God,
>
> — Romans 3:23

> For the wages of sin is death, but the gift of God is
> eternal life in Christ Jesus our Lord.
>
> — Romans 6:23

God loves you, and He desires for you to live abundantly here on earth, with purpose and conviction, AND with Him for eternity in Heaven after you leave this earth.

If you are ready, ask with all your heart for God to forgive your sins, accept what Jesus did on the Cross for you, and ask for and receive new life in the Holy Spirit.

Not sure how to pray? Here is a simple prayer:

Dear Lord Jesus, I know that I am a sinner, and I ask for Your forgiveness. I believe You died for my sins and rose from the dead. I turn from my sins and invite You to come into my heart and life. I want to trust and follow You as my Lord and Savior.

If you've just prayed to become a disciple of Jesus, welcome to the family! Scripture says angels in heaven are rejoicing over your salvation.

> In the same way, I tell you, there is rejoicing in the
> presence of the angels of God over one sinner
> who repents.
>
> — Luke 15:10

And God is beaming, arms open wide to welcome you

into His embrace. Take some time to thank Him for what He's done for you and enjoy His presence. Ask the Holy Spirit to guide you to a local Bible-teaching church where you can proclaim what you've done and begin your journey with other disciples of Jesus who can encourage and support you.

Maybe you are already a disciple. This book can remind you of the basics we all need to grow in spiritual fitness: a Bible, habits of repentance and forgiveness, time in His Word and in prayer, guidance from the Holy Spirit, and a desire to continuously move from the world's way to God's way in our daily lives.

Maybe you're not a disciple and not yet ready to pray and become one. That was me at one point in my life – notice that I did not give my life to Jesus until almost two years after I received a Bible and started reading it. I encourage you to keep seeking. Read the Bible. Read this book and see what God may speak to you as you read. Ask questions, to God and to others who know Jesus. God loves it when we ask questions. He is always by your side, always revealing Himself to you and waiting for you to respond. But again, realize that growing in one's faith and in a relationship with God without ever choosing to become a disciple of Jesus is just as impossible as growing in physical stature without ever having been born.

Maybe you don't believe in God at all, and you're surprised you read this far. I invite you to read further and ask God to reveal Himself to you. If you seriously want to know God, He will reveal Himself to you...and reveal His plans for your life.

> "For I know the plans I have for you," declares the Lord,
> "plans to prosper you and not to harm you,
> plans to give you hope and a future.
> Then you will call on me and come and pray to me,
> and I will listen to you.
> You will seek me and find me
> when you seek me with all your heart."
>
> — Jeremiah 29:11-13

As God has shown me and is longing to show you, He does a much better job of running our lives than we ever could. Give Him your all, and He'll give you His.

I can promise you will not be disappointed. Let's pray!

Dear Jesus,

I am seeking to fill the emptiness inside. I am tired of struggling, tired of pretending everything is OK when inside I'm hurting. I want to be at peace – if You are the way, please help my unbelief. I'm ready for a testimony of my own. So please come into my heart and take over my life. I invite You in – to be my Lord and Savior. Show me how to live for You!

In Your name I pray, Amen.

What the Bible says about following Jesus
(all verses from AMPC)

...all have sinned and are falling short of the honor and glory which God bestows and receives.

— Romans 3:23

For the wages which sin pays is death, but the [bountiful] free gift of God is eternal life through (in union with) Jesus Christ our Lord.

— Romans 6:23

Because if you acknowledge and confess with your lips that Jesus is Lord and in your heart believe (adhere to, trust in, and rely on the truth) that God raised Him from the dead, you will be saved.

For with the heart a person believes (adheres to, trusts in, and relies on Christ) and so is justified (declared righteous, acceptable to God), and with the mouth he confesses (declares openly and speaks out freely his faith) and confirms [his] salvation.

— Romans 10:9-10

For it is by free grace (God's unmerited favor) that you are saved (delivered from judgment and made partakers of Christ's salvation) through [your] faith. And this [salvation] is not of yourselves [of your own doing, it came not through your own striving], but it is the gift of God;

Not because of works [not the fulfillment of the Law's demands], lest any man should boast. [It is not the result of what anyone can possibly do, so no one can pride himself in it or take glory to himself.]

For we are God's [own] handiwork (His workmanship), recreated in Christ Jesus, [born anew] that we may do those good works which God predestined (planned beforehand) for us [taking paths which He prepared ahead of time], that we should walk in them [living the good life which He prearranged and made ready for us to live].

— Ephesians 2:8-10

For God has not appointed us to [incur His] wrath [He did not select us to condemn us], but [that we might] obtain [His] salvation through our Lord Jesus Christ (the Messiah)

Who died for us so that whether we are still alive or are dead [at Christ's appearing], we might live together with Him *and* share His life.

— 1 Thessalonians 5:9-10

Become a Disciple of Jesus   31

And this is the message [the message of promise] which we have heard from Him and now are reporting to you: God is Light, and there is no darkness in Him at all [no, not in any way].

[So] if we say we are partakers together and enjoy fellowship with Him when we live and move and are walking about in darkness, we are [both] speaking falsely and do not live and practice the Truth [which the Gospel presents].

But if we [really] are living and walking in the Light, as He [Himself] is in the Light, we have [true, unbroken] fellowship with one another, and the blood of Jesus Christ His Son cleanses (removes) us from all sin and guilt [keeps us cleansed from sin in all its forms and manifestations].

If we say we have no sin [refusing to admit that we are sinners], we delude and lead ourselves astray, and the Truth [which the Gospel presents] is not in us [does not dwell in our hearts].

If we [freely] admit that we have sinned and confess our sins, He is faithful and just (true to His own nature and promises) and will forgive our sins [dismiss our lawlessness] and [continuously] cleanse us from all unrighteousness [everything not in conformity to His will in purpose, thought, and action].

If we say (claim) we have not sinned, we contradict His Word and make Him out to be false and a liar, and His Word is not in us [the divine message of the Gospel is not in our hearts].

— 1 John 1:5-10

PLANNING
PREPARE TO LIVE DIFFERENTLY

Chapter 3
Recognize Your Responsibility

Never before has our culture legitimized such a mentality of entitlement. Personal responsibility and accountability are viewed as archaic. I could go on and on with examples, but if you've seen any news or spent any time on social media, you already know what I'm talking about. Many are living under a victim mentality that excuses them from having to be responsible for their lives, their place in life, their actions, their health, and most of all, their choices. It's always someone else's fault.

Twice in John (5:1-14, healing of the paralytic man at the pool of Bethsaida; and 8:1-11, forgiveness of the woman caught in adultery), Jesus said, "Go and sin no more." Jesus expected those He healed and forgave to change something about their lives so they would not get to that sinful place again. It was not a request on His part, it was a command. And Jesus never commands us to do that which we are unable to do.

I've heard people say, "I can't help it; if there's food in

the house, I'll eat it." Or, "But you don't know what I've been through." Or, "If you had to live with him (or her), you'd drink too." Behind each statement is the foundational belief that their actions are not their fault. In each case, they have proudly made themselves victims of something outside their control.

I, too, have tried to skirt responsibility with statements like, "But if they didn't say _____, I wouldn't have been *forced* to say _____." Or, "They do it too!" Or, "It's just the way I am." Truth is, those statements are just excuses—ways to justify in our minds the poor choices we are making. Instead of rising and declaring, "I can do this," we hide behind self-defeating statements that will keep us where we are. It is no different than someone who says, "I just can't seem to lose weight and get in shape," as they stuff another brownie in their mouth while sitting on the couch watching TV. We'd all see the futility in that, and can easily see that they are choosing to stay where they are.

But of course, *our* situation is always different.

Our society has glamorized being a victim and, thus, encourages us to blame someone or something else for our actions and choices. Instead of facing consequences, those who commit crimes and break the law are excused as victims of hard and abusive lives. Instead of seeking justice and being glad when justice is given, we are seduced into feeling sorry for them. After all, "they can't help it."

Or can they?

I might have been abused, but it's my choice if I continue to abuse others. I might have developed bad habits with my health, my speech, or my attitude, but when right actions are revealed to me, it's my choice if I continue the bad habits in my life instead of making a change. We hear wonderful stories of how people have risen out of amazingly hard circumstances and made something of their lives. What makes these people different? I believe it is simply their resolve to take responsibility for their lives and make the required choices and sacrifices to succeed. They have no more opportunity—and in many cases, much less opportunity—than others. They earn success because of what they do with what they have.

Many times in my marriage, I blamed my behavior problems on Don. If only he would change and be nicer, for example, I would not have to nag him. Or, the proverbial, "he started it!" (If you're married, I imagine you're nodding right now.) But Scripture is clear that we are to love—it is our choice, and our responsibility, regardless of what someone else does. So I could continue to nag and get frustrated, or choose to seek God to make changes in me so I could be more loving toward Don—I could choose to change and grow. I'm making progress; some days are better than others.

So let me ask you, are there areas in which you've allowed yourself to live as a victim? Have you abdicated responsibility for your actions?

Without the decision to change, you can read books like this one, ask for prayer, and plan all you want—but your efforts will only lead to frustration. God will continue to pursue and encourage you, but the action remains yours to take. No one can force change upon you. Others have tried that with me, and I with them. The result is always the same: frustrating failure.

Maybe as you read you still find yourself with reasons running through your mind about why you *can't* do this. Or maybe you can't see how change is possible but you'd like to change if you could. If that's the case, I encourage you to keep reading and ask the Lord to speak to you where you need it most. Yes, you *can* do this. God will meet you right where you are, just ask Him.

God loves all of us, and it's because of His great love that He gave us free will. We can choose to make excuses for why our lives aren't what we want them to be and remain unchanged, or we can choose to take responsibility for making our lives better.

Dear Jesus,

Please show me the areas in which I most need to change. Help me take responsibility for my choices in health, in my spiritual life, and in my relationships. Show me where I make excuses that are stopping me from making good choices. I know I can't change everything all at once, but I want to start with what's most important to You. Please show me what that is. I'm ready to change!

In Your name I pray, Amen.

Chapter 4
Determine Your Goal

Once we make the choice to accept responsibility, the next step is to set a goal. One reason fitness plans often fail is that we have unrealistic or faulty goals. For example, let's say we have been lazy and unfit for 10 years, yet we expect to run a marathon within a month. Or, we have a goal to "look like Joe/Jane"—someone who is naturally slender—when our bodies are not, no matter the amount of exercise and nutritional eating. Or, most dangerous of all, we just want to be smaller so we starve ourselves and run after quick fixes to obtain a look that is fleeting at best. We want the approval of others, and looking good often makes us think we have that approval.

Instead of these superficial goals, our goal with fitness should be overall health and well-being—to be the best we can be regardless of what that may look like on the outside. When we are properly focused, our slimming waistline and how well we feel will be natural by-products of better overall health. Any gains achieved by confusing the goal with the by-products are short-lived and will ultimately fail.

Spiritually speaking, we also set ourselves up for failure with the wrong goal. We desire to look good on the outside instead of allowing God to really change us on the inside. We set goals to act and look godlier so others will approve and accept us, or we desire to know more about God so we can make decisions we think He would make without needing to depend on Him. Once again, we are focused on ourselves. Instead, our goal should be to *love* God, *obey* Him, and *trust* Him with all that we are, all that we have, and all that we do *so that* we can truly love others. When that is our goal, we will naturally become more like Him on the inside where it counts, and our decisions will become naturally more like His decisions.

When we confuse the goal with the by-product, we become judgmental and angry. And, worse yet, we remain unchanged.

There was a time when I had no joy as a disciple of Jesus, and I was totally worn out from trying to do everything I read in the New Testament—be kind, gentle, patient, loving, and holy as He is holy, and so on. I made my own spiritual growth an idol, and worked hard to feed that idol. But only when I continually give up my own fleshly efforts am I able to walk in His love and experience His peace and joy. We must remember the truth that right standing with God comes only through Jesus, not through our actions. Then the doing becomes natural, as it is an extension of our spiritual selves that is guided every moment by the Holy Spirit, flowing from a life lived in simple obedience.

The goal for all of us is to continue moving toward loving our Lord and Savior more every day, and to reflect that love by obeying His commands by the power of His Holy Spirit. The goal is *not* performing His commands in our own power to earn His love and approval…although I sometimes slip back into trying to earn God's approval if I lose focus or discipline. My logic wants to make sense of a concept that only the Holy Spirit within me can understand, and sometimes it wins. Thankfully all I need to do is repent and receive God's forgiveness and I'm right back on track.

So I ask you now, what is your goal for wanting to become spiritually fit? Is it so that you can look good or become God over areas of your life? Or is it so that you can better love and serve God and, therefore, love and serve your family, friends, and co-workers? Becoming godlier in character is a by-product of a life lived in obedience to Him, but acting godly to appear godly should never be our goal.

Dear Jesus,

Please help me pursue the right goal for growing my faith. I want to grow closer to You every day, and learn how to keep peace in the midst of a crazy world. Please show me how to keep the right focus, and help me get quickly back on track when I stray toward the wrong goal or I am wrongly motivated. Help me set aside anything that is in the way of our relationship.

In Your name I pray, Amen.

Chapter 5
Resolve to Act

With your goal in mind, let's look at another important area of preparation: deciding to make a change *with resolve to act*.

Have you ever started an exercise program? You join the gym and the staff leads you on a tour of the exciting new world of shiny equipment that can transform your body in just a few short months. Your eyes light up and you set your mind saying, "This time it *will* work. I *will* come to the gym. I *will* make the time." For the first few weeks, all is going well. You are motivated to make your schedule work, and nothing stands in your way.

Then it starts to get a little old—same time, same routine, same equipment. What was once shiny and new becomes bothersome and mundane. Concurrently, the busyness of life sets in. Kids need rides to soccer practice and help with their homework. And well, they need to eat.

The "special project" at work requires you to work overtime. You miss one day at the gym, but you vow that you'll get back at it the next time. Then a friend calls and says, "Let's go do something fun," or one of the kids gets sick and needs your attention. Before you know it, you've missed several weeks and your resolve is completely eaten away. The underlying guilt turns into complete apathy. Who cares anyway?

Been there, done that, have a closet full of t-shirts! I can't tell you how many different gyms, programs, and workout centers I've joined and how much home equipment I've cycled through over the past 20 years. Each time I started, my resolve gave me the motivation to make time in my schedule. And each time, I enjoyed tangible results like increased energy and decreased weight.

But also each time, the infamous "something" caused me to fall away and lapse back into my fitness-less life. I knew I needed to be working out—and I knew there had to be something that would work. I tried aerobics classes, walking with a friend, and even hiring a personal trainer. These solutions all worked better than exercising alone because I had someone waiting for me and expecting me to show up.

But even then, the classes ended, friends moved or their schedules changed, and the training sessions ended (unless you have unlimited funding, which I didn't). Once again it was back to just me, alone, responsible for making the required changes. I seldom succeeded past the struggle because it was easier to sit back and do nothing than to make the effort to change.

So what is the solution? Where can we find endless motivation?

What I really need is someone to do the exercising for me. Wouldn't it be awesome if we could make the choice to be fit and then it would just happen? Of course, that's silly. Imagine saying, "Hey, my friends Jenny and Kathleen are helping me out. They are going to the gym for me so I can lose weight." You'd laugh and ask me, "What planet are you living on?"

We all know that no one else can exercise or eat right for us. It really is up to us. In fact, if someone tells us they intend to lose weight and bulk up but have no plans to eat differently or exercise, we'd question their sanity.

About six years ago, I knew I needed to get back to some type of exercise. I felt horrible, and I was at the age where exercise is increasingly important for continued mobility. I found CrossFit and have been doing it ever since. With the exception of a few weeks here and there due to needed sabbaticals, I have been able to consistently work out 3-4 times per week. I am in better shape now in my 60s than I've ever been in my life!

More recently I realized my eating also had to change or I'd never lose weight, have lower blood pressure, or sleep as well as I could. Yes, I exercised, but then ate so much that I could never get ahead. I'm only a short time into a new eating style, but so far, so good—I am reaping the benefits of losing weight and sleeping better.

So what changed? Why am I finally seeing success after so much failure?

Like others who exercise regularly and eat well, I

made a decision *with resolve* that health needed to be a priority. I had to "just do it." And I have to continue doing it. Other components of success I've seen in others, and in my own life, are:

- Find the exercise that is right for you – fits your schedule, your personality, and your ability.
- Make a plan and *discipline yourself* to follow through.
- Be intentional in your effort to be healthy so you reap the benefits in quality of life.
- If you must temporarily take a break due to life's circumstances, or miss a time or two of working out, or choose to enjoy a slice of cheesecake, don't let that sidetrack you for long.
- Develop a mindset that life is missing something *without* exercise.

Like physical fitness, the same principles are true for becoming spiritually fit. We must first make the decision that we want and need to be spiritually fit and closer to God. We must have the goal that our relationship with God is a priority in our lives. We must decide *with resolve* that we want to live our lives *His* way and not our own. We must decide that bringing the Kingdom of God to this earth is the meaning of our lives—not being happy. We must train ourselves and our beliefs (and remember no one else can do it for us) through daily practice, changing habits, and retraining how we think about everything in our lives.

It's not a one-time change; it's a new lifestyle. Let's pray!

Dear Jesus,

Please strengthen my resolve to grow spiritually and be closer to You. Help me become more disciplined in all areas of my life. Please help me find my tribe: those who are serious about growing closer to You. Help me set the right priorities and let go of anything in the way.

In Your name I pray, Amen.

BASIC TRAINING
MAINTAIN YOUR FOUNDATION

Chapter 6
Read the Bible

The key to the success of every fitness plan is the equipment used for the workout. Spiritually, that equipment starts with the Word of God, aka Scripture, aka the Bible. God gave us a few verses to help us understand the importance of Scripture and why we need to study it.

The Bible shows us the condition of our hearts.

> For the word of God is alive and active. Sharper than any double-edged sword, it penetrates even to dividing soul and spirit, joints and marrow; it judges the thoughts and attitudes of the heart.
>
> — Hebrews 4:12

The Bible teaches us and equips us.

> All Scripture is God-breathed and is useful for teaching, rebuking, correcting and training in righteousness, so that the servant of God may be thoroughly equipped for every good work.
>
> — 2 Timothy 3:16-17

The Bible reveals Jesus to us.

> In the beginning was the Word, and the Word was with God, and the Word was God. He was with God in the beginning. Through him all things were made; without him nothing was made that has been made. In him was life, and that life was the light of all mankind. The light shines in the darkness, and the darkness has not overcome it.
>
> — John 1:1-5

The Bible shows us how to live in truth and freedom.

> To the Jews who had believed him, Jesus said, "If you hold to my teaching, you are really my disciples. Then you will know the truth, and the truth will set you free."
>
> — John 8:31-32

God has written us a love story about His great love for us, culminating in the sacrifice of His Son Jesus so that we can spend eternity with Him. The Bible is full of stories about real people with real problems and sometimes horrible sinfulness and pride. Time and again, God rescued them when they cried out to Him for help, even when they didn't deserve it. The Bible also includes stories about people who experienced God's discipline and suffered lifelong consequences of their choices, also a result of God's great love and mercy.

In the Bible, God reveals Himself, His character, and His ways. He is consistent, perfect in love and holiness, never changing, slow to anger, and rich in mercy. He refers to Himself as I AM, Healer, Provider, Jehovah, Deliverer, Alpha and Omega, Beginning and End, Love, Truth, Light and so many other names (for a fun study, Google "names of God" and see all the results!)

As Jesus, He is Savior and Redeemer, and the only way we can have a relationship with God.

> Jesus answered, "I am the way and the truth and the life. No one comes to the Father except through me."
>
> — John 14:6

As the Holy Spirit, He is Counselor, Helper, and Advocate.

> But the Advocate, the Holy Spirit, whom the Father will send in my name, will teach you all things and will remind you of everything I have said to you.
>
> — John 14:26

God's wisdom and justice are incomparable to anyone or anything. Yet with all He reveals about Himself in His Word, we will never come close to fully understanding Who He is in all of His glory. The more I learn about Him, the more I realize how little I know in comparison to all that He is. And yet as He becomes magnified to me (and so much larger than I ever imagined), I rest more securely in knowing that a truly Almighty and Sovereign God is my Father.

When we don't know what God's Word says about Him, we often view Him through filters based on how our earthly fathers treated us, or based on what others say about Him. We tend to fear Him, judge Him, and think of Him as "way up there" and unconcerned about us. Because we tend to think that, instead of running into His outstretched arms to receive His love and help, we shrink away from Him in fear of judgment and condemnation. Instead of trusting and obeying Him, we make our own plans and go our own way.

His love story also includes abundant words of truth about us and about how God sees us. His Word says we are His beloved, His creation, His children, and we are acceptable in His sight. The way He made us is good. The way we behave may not always be good, but inside where our identity lies, we are good because we are His, and He has given us the righteousness of Jesus in exchange for our sin. We are a new creation, nothing can separate us from God's love, and we can love others because He loves us.

> Therefore, if anyone is in Christ, the new creation has come: The old has gone, the new is here! All this is from God, who reconciled us to himself through Christ and gave us the ministry of reconciliation: that God was reconciling the world to himself in Christ, not counting people's sins against them. And he has committed to us the message of reconciliation. We are therefore Christ's ambassadors, as though God were making his appeal through us. We implore you on Christ's behalf: Be reconciled to God. God made him who had no sin to be sin for us, so that in him we might become the righteousness of God.
>
> — 2 Corinthians 5:17-21

We love because he first loved us.

— 1 John 4:19

> For I am convinced that neither death nor life,
> neither angels nor demons, neither the present
> nor the future, nor any powers, neither height
> nor depth, nor anything else in all creation, will
> be able to separate us from the love of God that
> is in Christ Jesus our Lord.
>
> — Romans 8:38-39

When we don't know what His Word says about us, we tend to compare ourselves to others, leading to either judgment of them when they don't measure up or envy because we perceive them as being better than us. We fruitlessly try to change ourselves to what we think we should be, again with the wrong goal (to look good on the outside or gain others' approval). We live in condemnation, beating ourselves up every time we make a mistake. We strive and strain to *become* instead of resting in the truth of God's Word that we already *are.*

We need to allow the truth of the Bible to define God and define us—not the opinions of others, our experiences, our jobs, our families, our possessions, or our position in life. In true humility, we can allow God to change us, and we'll begin to see others through His eyes.

Reading the Bible also helps us recognize right from wrong according to how God designed us to live. When we hear or think something and we're not sure if it's God or not, we can test it by whether the Bible confirms or contradicts what we've heard. While we may not always get an absolute confirmation, we know that if we find a contradiction, then what we've heard is not the truth and therefore it was not spoken by God. For example, the Bible says that God is love and that He loves us with an everlasting love. So if we hear a voice, in our heads or from someone else, that says, "God could never love you" or "You'll never be good enough for God's love," we know we've heard a lie.

The Bible also helps us to keep the right perspective on what's really important: our eternal lives. When we regularly read the Bible, many things in our daily lives seem so much less important in the big scheme of eternity. And our confidence in God grows such that whatever we see going on around us cannot steal our peace.

While not necessary, it's helpful to invest in a study Bible with notes, application sections, and a concordance (verse search by key word) in a translation you can understand. The websites www.Biblegateway.com, www.Crosswalk.com, and https://bible.org/ contain a wealth of study helps, including tools that function like a concordance. The great value of a word-search concordance is that it allows you to search for verses that contain specific words. For example, if you want to study about "mercy," looking up "mercy" in the concordance will identify relevant verses.

Reading the Bible isn't just one of those checklist things to do. And the purpose of reading the Bible is not to just know *about* God and fill up with intellectual knowledge, or to be able to know the "rules" so we can live by following some type of formula. Rather, it is a way of getting to know who God is, how He thinks, and what He has to say about us and our place in the world *so that* we can live as God created us to live every day, in the fullness of relationship with Him, obediently following His ways and learning His voice. Only through continued obedience to His truth can we grow in our understanding so that we correctly decipher the world around us and our place in it.

Without reading the Bible with that intent, we cannot know God, period.

Dear Jesus,

Please help me make reading Your Word a priority in my life. Help me find the time of day it's best for me to read. I want to understand the truth I read in the Bible about You and Your love for me, and about how I can grow as Your disciple. I ask for wisdom, understanding, and an increase in faith as I learn more about You. Please guide me to the Bible translations and study materials I need. Help me fall in love with Your Word.

In Your name I pray, Amen.

Chapter 7
Repent From Your Sins

Many times, I sin in the same area over and over and over again. I confess that I'm sorry. And then I sin again and can't understand why I don't do better. One time the Lord showed me why: my "repentance" stops with my apology because of my unbelief.

While I usually feel badly about what I've done and want to do better, deep down inside I don't believe I can do it. So when I sin yet again, I apologize but immediately focus on myself and my inability to change. I droop my shoulders and resign myself, thinking, *Oh well, maybe I will do better next time.* This self-focused attitude gives Satan, the enemy of our souls, a foothold to keep us under condemnation.

We can read the Bible all day long, but without true repentance the words are empty. Many people want to live as a disciple of Jesus, but fail at it because they either don't understand repentance or are not willing to do what is required. They say, "I believe Jesus died on the Cross for my sins," but they never change—their daily lives and character show little evidence of that belief.

So what is true repentance?

In Matthew 3:8, Jesus instructs us to:

> "prove by the way you live that you have really turned from your sins and turned to God" (NLT);
> "produce fruit in keeping with repentance." (NIV)

Dictionary.com says to *repent* is "to feel sorry, self-reproachful, or contrite for past conduct; regret or be conscience-stricken about a past action, attitude, etc."[1] Overall, repentance requires being remorseful and sorry about what you did. Biblical repentance goes a step further than this dictionary definition. According to Easton's 1897 Bible Dictionary, "evangelical repentance" consists of

1. a true sense of one's own guilt and sinfulness;
2. an apprehension of God's mercy in Christ;
3. an actual hatred of sin (Psalm 119:128; Job 42:5, 6; 2 Corinthians 7:10) and turning from it to God; and
4. a persistent endeavour after a holy life in walking with God in the way of His commandments.[2]

In other words, we must not only be sorry, but we must turn resolutely from our ways and go in a whole new direction...including what we think and the motives behind our actions. Jesus addressed this topic with the Pharisees more than once.

> "You brood of vipers, how can you who are evil say anything good? For the mouth speaks what the heart is full of. A good man brings good things out of the good stored up in him, and an evil man brings evil things out of the evil stored up in him."
>
> — Matthew 12:34-35

> "Woe to you, teachers of the law and Pharisees, you hypocrites! You clean the outside of the cup and dish, but inside they are full of greed and self-indulgence. Blind Pharisee! First clean the inside of the cup and dish, and then the outside also will be clean.
> "Woe to you, teachers of the law and Pharisees, you hypocrites! You are like whitewashed tombs, which look beautiful on the outside but on the inside are full of the bones of the dead and everything unclean.
>
> — Matthew 23:25-27

Jesus uses strong language to point out that while they might look good on the outside to themselves and the people, the motives of their hearts were sinful. They needed to repent.

To help with understanding what repentance requires and what can often get in the way for all of us, I've used the word *repent* as an acronym to share what I've learned (and what I'm still learning).

R – REALIZE that you've sinned. Be willing to admit not just that you've made a mistake, but that you've sinned. Stop justifying. Call sin exactly what it is—sin. The Lord once impressed upon me the following truth: *If you don't call it sin, you can't take it to the Cross.* The Cross has no power over rationalizing, reasoning, or justifying what we've done if we're not fully acknowledging that we've sinned. We need to ask the Lord to show us His perspective on what we've done—to see how our words or behavior have hurt Him and/or hurt the person against whom we've sinned. With God's help, we need to identify the sin we've committed. Have we failed to love? Have we spoken hurtful words of gossip or slander or judgment? Have we acted out of greed or envy? Or have we realized we've sinned but then tried to cover it up?

The word *sin* often causes people to cringe and then try to justify themselves. Even though sin is referenced all through the Bible, along with every person's propensity toward sin, too many times we cannot accept that the *all* in verses like "For *all* have sinned…" includes us. Thus, when we sin, we rationalize and reason and make excuses rather than *admit* that we've sinned.

Repent From Your Sins 63

But the Bible makes it clear that we need to confess sin to be forgiven.

Proverbs 28:13 states:

"Whoever conceals their sins does not prosper, but the one who confesses and renounces them finds mercy."

First John 1:9 states:

"If we confess our sins, he is faithful and just and will forgive us our sins and purify us from all unrighteousness."

If we haven't sinned, what is there to forgive? We block the flow of grace and mercy into our lives by trying to cover up our sin with excuses or reasoning like, "It's not that bad," or "Is it really wrong to do that?" or "I know it was wrong, but…" With these justifications, we deny the value and power of the Cross.

Why? Because we put our identity in the sin, or even the lack of sin, instead of in who we are in Christ and in who we are according to God's Word. We don't understand how to balance the seemingly conflicting truths that we are all unworthy to receive God's love, yet we are so valuable and loved by God that Jesus died for us. Because we don't understand, we think that our behavior, right or wrong, is influencing God's love for us; therefore, we can't admit sin because then God wouldn't be able to love us. We stay trapped, condemned, and hopeless instead of trusting what God says about us in His Word, including how much He loves us and how our identity is in Jesus alone.

E – EMBRACE responsibility for what you've done. How many times do we get the first part right and call it sin, but then continue to say how it's not really our fault? To fully experience forgiveness and for the Cross to be effective, we must be willing to accept full responsibility for our actions. Are there sometimes outside factors? Yes. But it's always our choice to allow them to influence us or to blame them (or another person) for why we did what we did.

A typical example of this is being late for an appointment with someone. Being late in and of itself may not be a sin, but the result of being late is that we disrespect the other person by not valuing their time. Yes, sometimes we may be late due to a traffic jam that's not our fault, but are we sorry we're late for how it affected the other person, or do we just throw that in as part of the explanation? I am definitely a work in progress in this area—I am often running behind schedule for one reason or another. For example, when I plan to meet someone at 8:30 and that means I need to leave my house at 8 a.m., I may fiddle and putter and tidy up here and there, right up until 7:50, and *then* get in the shower when I suddenly realize the time. It is a selfish mindset to not be conscious of the time; therefore, I am violating the simple law of love. My apology goes something like this, "So sorry I'm late, but I got distracted with stuff around the house." It's humbling to realize as I write this that I'm often just spitting out the words I've been trained to say, expecting understanding and forgiveness when I'm not really sorry at all.

It's especially hard for me to embrace responsibility for my own sin when what I say or do is in reaction to someone else's sinful behavior. For example, when someone treats me wrongfully, my natural reaction is to respond in the same way. Can you relate? Fortunately, I have a very wise and loving friend who is not afraid to tell me, "Yes, I know they hurt you and I'm sorry, but how did you respond?" She correctly points out (and has done so many times) that it doesn't matter what anyone else says or does. My only responsibility is for my own words and actions. Another person's sin can never be an excuse for me to sin in return.

Other ways we justify include saying things like:

- "Sorry I reacted angrily, but that's a weak spot in me that the Lord is working on."
- "Sorry I forgot your birthday, but I've just been so busy lately."
- "Sorry I hurt you, but _____ (fill in the blank)."

My sister-in-law once told me that she realized saying "Sorry, but..." totally invalidated the apology. We're not really sorry; instead, we're explaining why we messed up —justifying what we did and then trying to sell it to the other person so they are not mad or disappointed with us. Our concern is not really about them, but about ourselves and how they see us.

P – PRAY. Pray to ask for forgiveness, pray to bless the other person, pray for God's mercy and grace to cover your sin. Pray to forgive yourself. Get alone with God and take it all to Him, being completely honest with Him and with yourself—He knows it anyway. Then choose to speak words of life. Receive by faith His forgiveness, His love, and His peace.

In the case of someone else's offense triggering a sinful response in you, you also need to pray to forgive them and bless them. When you do, the Lord can work in their life in ways you cannot, no matter what you say or do.

Most of all, pray for God's grace to enable you to stay on the right path. Sadly, sins can become bad habits and, as such, need to be broken. Pray for the Lord to soften your conscience in that area and for Him to quickly and firmly convict you when you step off the path.

This continues to be an area of struggle for me and a big waste of time. Often my prayers start with all my excuses of why I acted the way I did, then I move on to how it was not really my fault, and then eventually I end with my admittance of guilt and request for forgiveness. I also plot and plan how I am going to "fix" everything and make it right. This is wrong. While I need to accept responsibility for my sin and sometimes suffer consequences or make retribution, I don't need to eternally "pay" for what I've done. Neither do you, nor does anyone. Jesus already did that.

We also don't need to carry the guilt or burden into tomorrow, or rehash the event again and again. Pray for help to let go and move on.

E – EXPECT consequences to continue. We may be forgiven and truly changed, but the effects of our sinful actions often linger. We find this surprising and often take offense when we're misunderstood, or when someone doesn't immediately respond in ways we think they should. If we break someone's trust by sharing something told to us in confidence, that person may not be willing to share anything else with us that is confidential. If we judge someone and act toward someone out of that judgment, he or she may not want to be around us or may not speak warmly toward us. If we lie to someone, that person may not readily believe what we say the next time.

I've experienced this with my husband, Don. The Lord has been continually working on my heart in the areas of how I judge him and how I show (or don't show) him respect with my words. Often the disrespect and judgment are reflected in *how* I say the words rather than in the specific words themselves. As the Lord has been changing my heart, my behavior has reflected more respect and admiration for Don. While he immediately noticed the change, he also continued to react to certain words or phrases even though the intent and tone behind them was completely different. For example, "Can you please turn down the TV?" evoked the response, "Yes, boss," because previously my tone made those seven words sound like, "I can't believe you're even watching TV. I can't stand the TV. Why do you have to watch it at all, let alone have it so loud?" I felt the change on the inside and knew I had just made a simple request, but when Don heard those words, they still triggered the old response. At first, I became defensive and many arguments ensued; but because I had truly repented and God had changed my heart, eventually Don's reactions mirrored the way the words were spoken.

N – NO MORE! The enemy will continue to tempt us where we have repented, especially where our sins turned into bad habits. Old habits are hard to break, like my habitually running late. I set alarms, set reminders on my phone, and resolve to get better. Still, I sometimes can't seem to get out the door on time. Yes, well, I need to read what I just wrote and pray for Jesus to strengthen my resolve in this area!

Another difficult-to-break and all-too-common habit is gossip. Someone may feel guilty about gossiping and resolve to stop. Then they don't necessarily *repeat stories* but find themselves speaking negatively about someone else.

When the Lord brings conviction (guilty feeling) and correction, we must resolve to respond to His nudge and take action immediately, firmly, and *completely*. Someone once told me that being mostly obedient is still disobedience. We must be willing to do whatever it takes to continue to walk in our new, changed way.

One area in my life that gets a good workout here is judgmental thoughts. As I waited to have my nails done one day, I noticed a young girl sitting next to me with a blood red French manicure. (With a French manicure the tips of the nails are traditionally white; hers were red.) With a swift look at her, I saw that she wore her hair in her eyes, heavy make-up, and tight clothes. In my mind, I stereotyped her as a rebellious teenager. The man doing her nails had similar thoughts as evidenced by his conversation with her about dating. He talked to her about love and asked her what she thought it was. Much to my surprise and humiliation she said, "I believe what the Bible says about love—that's my guideline." I then looked more closely at her and noticed how sweetly she smiled and saw that her clothes were not *that* revealing. In fact, she simply dressed as a typical teenager.

And I felt like the proverbial slug.

I completely failed the "no more" part of repentance. Instead of firmly saying no to the first judgmental thought that came into my mind about her nails and asking God for *His* thoughts about her, I let my resolve slip and allowed the other judgmental thoughts free entry. Thankfully, the Lord humbled me when He let me see a little bit of her heart for Him; and I was able to smile at her and offer words of encouragement.

We also need to say "No more!" to condemnation. This includes quickly asking forgiveness, forgiving ourselves when we do slip up, and getting right back on track. It's easy to quit and beat ourselves up when we make a mistake, just like it's easy to quit working out when we miss a few days. But we can't become sidetracked from our goal—we need to get up and keep going! We must focus on our secure identity in Christ, not on the mistake.

T – TELL someone about it. Light and accountability are crucial to staying on the right path. Maybe the sin is something private, like looking at pornography. We realize it is sinful, embrace responsibility (yes, I visited that website), pray for forgiveness, and expect to continue with the struggle. We even say, "No more—I will not look at this ever again!" and we mean it. But then the temptations bombard us. *Hey, no one knows, and it's right here, and...* Before we know it, we've fallen again. Condemnation and shame thrive in that darkness, and they quickly barrage us with despair and hopelessness.

Telling another person and praying with them brings light, and it also brings Jesus front and center into the picture.

> For where two or three gather in my name, there am I with them.
>
> — Matthew 18:20

> Therefore confess your sins to each other and pray for each other so that you may be healed. The prayer of a righteous man is powerful and effective.
>
> — James 5:16

> Carry each other's burdens, and in this way you will fulfill the law of Christ.
>
> — Galatians 6:2

We need the acceptance of someone who loves us and knows our darkness, and the power of standing two together.

True repentance means making a 180-degree turn away from sin and moving resolutely in the opposite direction —shoulders back and head up, looking at Jesus. When we brace ourselves with feet firmly planted on the Rock, we send notice to the enemy of our souls (Satan) that we will not bend, we will not break, and we will not give in. We choose to believe and to act on this truth:

> I have strength for all things in Christ Who
>   empowers me
> [I am ready for anything and equal to anything
> through Him Who infuses inner strength into me;
> I am self-sufficient in Christ's sufficiency].
>
> — Philippians 4:13 (AMPC)

We fix our eyes on Jesus and let His glory, love, power, and grace be magnified so that all else becomes dim. We can only be transformed on the inside if we are continually moving in ever-increasing repentance in more areas and to greater degrees in our lives. We choose to turn away from sin; God changes us.

Dear Jesus,

Please help me to identify and call out the sins in my own life—both in action and in my heart—and learn how to quickly repent and change direction. Help me to trust in Your grace and mercy, and be willing to confess my sin instead of making excuses and reasoning them away. Reveal any hidden sin in me so I can confess it and find mercy. Help me not to walk in guilt or shame—to trust Your Word that when I confess, You forgive completely.

In Your name I pray, Amen.

Chapter 8
Forgive as God Forgives You

Many others have written books about forgiveness that cover the topic in great detail. I am not a theologian; my goal is to share a few things Jesus said, and what I've learned in my walk with Jesus, to help you understand that forgiveness is foundational to our lives as Christians.

The Gospel of Matthew contains several references to forgiveness, spoken by Jesus Himself. In the primary verses from chapter 6, Jesus ends the Lord's prayer with the following declaration:

> "For if you forgive other people when they sin against you, your heavenly Father will also forgive you. But if you do not forgive others their sins, your Father will not forgive your sins."
>
> — Matthew 6:14-15

Jesus did not leave room for negotiation. No "unless" exemption clause; e.g., unless they intentionally hurt you, unless they betrayed you, unless what they did can never be made right on this earth. Those are the very things that we *must* forgive. Jesus made it clear that forgiveness applies to *all* sin, including intentional and willfully deliberate actions as well as what is done unintentionally.

Like with repentance, you also can't forgive what you don't admit was a sin against you. For example, a friend once hurt me deeply with her mean and bullying words and actions. Instead of acknowledging what she did as sin, and admitting the associated hurt, I pushed down the hurt and told myself, "well, she is hurting me out of her own wounded place, I understand." While that may be true, it's not the whole truth: my friend sinned against me, it hurt, I now need to forgive her and trust God to heal that hurt.

Then in Matthew 18, Jesus addresses how often we need to forgive.

> Then Peter came to Jesus and asked, "Lord, how many times shall I forgive my brother or sister who sins against me? Up to seven times?" Jesus answered, "I tell you, not seven times, but seventy times seven."
>
> — Matthew 18:21-22

For the math brains reading this, the answer to seventy times seven is 490. Maybe this means if someone does the same thing to you every day for well over a year, you are to forgive them every day. Or maybe it means that you need to keep forgiving someone by choice until you can love and bless them from your heart. Yes, sometimes forgiveness is a process. Overall, I believe what Jesus is saying by this is that we are to walk with forgiveness in our hearts toward those who hurt us, no matter how long it takes to get there. He's always after our heart attitudes, not our performance.

Jesus continues teaching with a parable about an unmerciful servant who is forgiven a great debt by his master, then turns around and refuses to forgive a small debt owed to him. The master hands the man over to the jailers to be tortured, then ends the parable with:

> "This is how my heavenly Father will treat each of you unless you forgive your brother or sister from your heart."
>
> — Matthew 18:35

There it is again: it's about our hearts. In Matthew 5, Jesus goes beyond actions that everyone would expect to bear consequences and addresses the heart attitude:

> "You have heard that it was said to the people long ago, 'You shall not murder, and anyone who murders will be subject to judgment.' But I tell you that anyone who is angry with a brother or sister will be subject to judgment. Again, anyone who says to a brother or sister, 'Raca,' is

> answerable to the court. And anyone who says, 'You fool!' will be in danger of the fire of hell."
>
> — Matthew 5:21-22

> "You have heard that it was said, 'You shall not commit adultery.' But I tell you that anyone who looks at a woman lustfully has already committed adultery with her in his heart."
>
> — Matthew 5:27-28

Jesus knows that what is in our hearts will heavily influence our actions. That's why we need to confess what is in our hearts, not just our wrong actions. It's from our hearts that we enjoy relationship with God and others. When we have something against someone, we often perform, pretend, and put on a happy face to hide our true feelings and keep the peace. We avoid contact with the person who hurt us so we can avoid dealing with our unforgiveness.

But that doesn't last long. When we continue in unforgiveness, we become increasingly empty and lonely on the inside, and increasingly angry and bitter both inside and out. All our relationships suffer, especially our relationship with God.

Sometimes I hold unforgiveness against my husband Don. Often I don't know it until it surfaces in other ways. Like, thinking nothing he does is right. Or I find a million things to do rather than spend time with him. Or I simply feel burdened, weary, sad, and angry about nothing in particular. That's when God starts trying to get my attention. When I finally go to Him, He shows me what I'm holding on to and helps me let it go and forgive. Peace returns.

So if you find yourself at odds with someone and don't know why, maybe you need to forgive them. God will help you, if you ask.

I've heard that forgiveness includes forgiving ourselves. I believe it's more that we need to fully receive God's forgiveness for our sins and not let our pride get in the way, or try to justify and reason away our sins. We can't give what we haven't received—impossible to forgive others if we judge ourselves so roughly that our own hearts are not full of God's mercy and love.

When we fully understand and receive God's forgiveness for our own sins, we can more graciously see others through God's eyes and forgive them. Just like our sin does not define us to God, neither should someone else's sin define them to us.

Forgiveness is made possible only through Jesus' death and resurrection. He could have taken out His wrath on us for our sins and completely destroyed us; we deserve it. Instead, He sent His son to earth to pay for our sins. *Our* sins, the corporate "our" that includes everyone. He's way more concerned about us being with Him forever so He made a way for that to happen.

He wants us to do the same toward / for others: be way more concerned that our friends, loved ones, and even our enemies have a chance to know His love and the forgiveness He bought for us. If we forgive someone when they know they don't deserve our forgiveness, we give them a taste of God's immeasurable mercy—the same mercy we received from God. When we forgive, we let go of our pains and hurts and let God heal them. We let go of the desire for vengeance and payback and trust God for His perfect justice.

God will enable us to forgive if we make the choice from our hearts and step out in faith. He commands us to forgive and never asks us to do anything that we are unable to do. It's not about what you feel, it's about what you choose to do. And as Jesus made so very clear, your eternal life with Him depends on your choice to forgive *all* those who sin against you.

I'd like to close with a short testimony that deepened my heart understanding of how true repentance and forgiveness can work together to preserve relationships.

Several years ago, Don and I sold our roofing business to a couple the Lord brought us whom we knew would run it with the same integrity. They have not only kept it going but have grown it to another level that we could not have envisioned. We are proud of what they built on the foundation we laid.

Last year they started doing more intensive marketing, including videos of the history of the company that talked about what Don and I had started and built. When their marketing person posted the video on social media, he mistakenly included language in the post that implied this couple were the original owners of the business. We (mostly me) jumped to the conclusion that they were trying to take credit for what we did. Intentionally misleading marketing!

Instead of (1) watching the video and seeing what it said, (2) believing the best, and (3) directly asking them about the post, we made a snarky comment on the post. She replied with "LOL" and took the post as a joke because she knew their intentions and that the video honored us. Then we judged that she was mocking us. Our judgment led to offense, our offense to anger, and anger to a hasty action: we left a voice mail for them about our outrage at their presumption and light-hearted treatment of our hurt.

In tears, they called us back. Our accusation hit them out of the blue because they thought our comment was intended to be funny. They didn't know what had been posted since someone else did it, and their goal has always been to honor us with the business they inherited from us. They didn't know what they could have done to upset us so much. I still get upset when I think about how wrong we were and how much we hurt them!

The four of us talked and cried through intense apologies, hurt hearts, and then forgiveness. When I say forgiveness, I mean in the truest sense of the word: as though it never happened. We humbled ourselves and took full ownership of rushing to judgment, and they extended God's mercy to us and forgave us. We honestly would have understood if it took a whole lot of time for them to get over it, if ever, because that's what we felt like we deserved. Instead, we received mercy: they showed us God's heart and it humbled us to the core.

We have had many conversations since that day, and this topic has never again come up. When both parties are willing to do their part, the miraculous result glorifies God in every way, and relationships are strengthened instead of destroyed. That's true forgiveness from the heart!

Sadly, both parties are not always willing to move forward in forgiveness. When that happens, rest assured that you are always forgiven by God when you confess. Learn from what happened. Apologize if you've wronged the other person and continue to pray for that person. Forgive the one who hurt you, even if they don't ask. The relationship may never be the same, but you can enjoy God's peace when you do as much as possible to live in peace with others (Romans 12:18). And when you forgive as Christ forgave you.

Dear Jesus,

Please show me anyone I need to forgive, and help me forgive them. Help me to receive Your forgiveness so I can give others forgiveness from my heart. Please help me process my emotions, and heal my heart from the hurts. I want to forgive everyone as You forgive me – completely and without looking back.

In Your name I pray, Amen.

LIFESTYLE

MAKE GOD A PRIORITY IN YOUR DAILY LIFE

Chapter 9
Grow in Intimacy with God

I once heard intimacy described as "into me see." We all long to be known fully and accepted as we are, warts and all. The more we reveal to another person, and they don't reject us, the closer we feel to them and the more confident we feel in being ourselves.

The safest Person with whom to start a journey of intimacy is God, our Father.

Depending on your background, the concept of being that close to a father may be terrifying! This is definitely one of those "you need to unlearn before learning" times. Our earthly fathers may have been loving or abusive; but either way they were far from perfect. They all made mistakes, hurt us, rejected us, or let us down at one time or another...whether intentionally or unintentionally.

But they are not God.

God is the perfect Father who is always for our good and never makes a mistake. It may take time for you to grasp this truth deeply in your souls—the truth that is foundational to everything else we learn about living as a disciple. So we invest daily in our relationship with God, and get to know Him more intimately as we choose to:

- Spend time alone with Him. Hide away from the noise and distractions of life. He will reveal Himself to you in ways that are amazingly perfect and gentle. He'll whisper thoughts of love—and correction—to you that are remarkably timed and perfect. He'll guide you to read verses in the Bible that are perfect for your current needs.

- Read the Bible. There is no substitute.

- Journal your thoughts, feelings, insights, prayers, and praises.

- Worship God. Sing to Him, focus on Him. Let God minister His peace, mercy, and love to your spirit as you listen to worship music written by others and reflect on the words of the songs. Or, write your own songs and psalms to God from your heart to His.

- Invest in relationships with other disciples. People can model God's mercy and grace to us. We learn by observing how they walk through tough situations. God also speaks directly to us through others in amazing ways. I've had friends come up to me out of the blue and say, "I was praying for you today, and God showed me _____." I am reduced to tears as they share something about me that only God knew…always something I needed to hear, and perfectly timed.

- Read devotional books. These are books with daily readings of encouragement and truth. I often read three or more devotions every day in addition to the Bible. I can't tell you how many times my devotional readings lined up perfectly with each other and with what God was speaking to my heart. God is so amazing! Not sure what to get? Look online or go to a local bookstore, and prayerfully browse the devotionals section.

These are three of my all-time favorite devotionals:
1. *My Utmost for His Highest* by Oswald Chambers[1]
2. *A Year with C.S. Lewis* by C.S. Lewis[2]
3. *Worship the King* by Chris Tiegreen[3]

Growing in intimacy with God and learning to fully trust Him is a process. God our Father is perfect in all His ways. He longs for you to know Him intimately and to share that personal time with you. And, news flash: He already knows every thought before you think it, how you feel, and the truth about your heart. He knows you better than you know yourself!

Maybe you're not sure what to do when you're alone

with God. Begin by going to a quiet place, turning off your phone and computer, and praying something like this: "Here I am, God. I am giving You this time so we can become closer. What do You have for me today?"

Listen and pay attention to seemingly random thoughts that come to your mind. Write down your thoughts and feelings as you focus on God. Ask Him questions about anything at all—He delights in conversation with you! Pray for your family, your friends, your church. If nothing specific comes to mind, read something in the Bible or read a devotional (or two). If your mind is racing with thoughts of the day ahead, jot down notes so you can handle those items after your time with Him.

With practice and persistence, alone time with God will become the highlight of your day. You won't know how you ever lived without it!

Dear Jesus,

Please help me make a realistic plan to invest in our relationship and grow closer to You. I don't know what I need or how much, but You do. Lead me to others who can journey along with me. Please show me how I can arrange my day so that we have time together. Reveal yourself to me, I want to know You more every day. Thank You, I love You!

In Your name I pray, Amen.

Chapter 10
Exchange the World's Ways for God's Ways

When working out at the gym, it's not uncommon to have someone review all of the equipment with you and help you determine which equipment will bring the most benefit. When it comes to eating right, you and I may consult books and other avenues that will help us know which food will be best. In both cases, we are looking to an expert who has experience and can guide us. If we do as they say, follow their principles and formulas, we'll enjoy physical transformation.

Spiritually, we have the Holy Spirit—the Counselor, Helper, and Guide—as our expert. We need to learn more about how to recognize His voice and follow His ways. If we do as He says, we'll enjoy spiritual transformation from the inside out.

Unlike physical fitness, though, following the Holy Spirit is not a listen-once-and-follow-the-formula discipline. It's a relationship. We walk with Him and converse with Him every day.

As we grow in intimacy with God, we learn more

88   Finding the Missing Something

about the Holy Spirit and how to recognize His voice. We also need to learn how to get things out of the way that interfere with His voice. This chapter focuses on three conditions in which we can be out of balance and, therefore, unable to hear God clearly:

1. We can be driven by our feelings and desires.
2. We want what we see, and we want it now.
3. We want to be in control so we don't need anyone or anything.

First John 2:16 names these problem areas the lust of the flesh, the lust of the eyes, and the pride of life. Read each of the following translations of 1 John 2:15-16. Notice the very clear contrast between the world and the love of Jesus.

The New International Version (NIV):

> Do not love the world or anything in the world. If anyone loves the world, the love of the Father is not in them. For everything in the world—the lust of the flesh, the lust of the eyes, and the pride of life—comes not from the Father but from the world.

The New Living Translation (NLT):

> Do not love this world nor the things it offers you, for when you love the world, you do not have the love of the Father in you. For the world

offers only a craving for physical pleasure, a craving for everything we see, and pride in our achievements and possessions. These are not from the Father, but are from this world.

The Message (MSG):

Don't love the world's ways. Don't love the world's goods. Love of the world squeezes out love for the Father. Practically everything that goes on in the world—wanting your own way, wanting everything for yourself, wanting to appear important—has nothing to do with the Father. It just isolates you from him. The world and all its wanting, wanting, wanting is on the way out—but whoever does what God wants is set for eternity.

The Amplified Bible (AMP):

Do not love or cherish the world or the things that are in the world. If anyone loves the world, love for the Father is not in him. For all that is in the world--the lust of the flesh [craving for sensual gratification] and the lust of the eyes [greedy longings of the mind] and the pride of life [assurance in one's own resources or in the stability of earthly things] – these do not come from the Father but are from the world [itself].

The New King James Version (NKJV):

> Do not love the world or the things in the world. If anyone loves the world, the love of the Father is not in him. For all that is in the world—the lust of the flesh, the lust of the eyes, and the pride of life—is not of the Father but is of the world.

In today's world, following Jesus and living like Jesus are incredibly difficult because we are constantly striving against the victim mentality and our selfish culture of entitlement. As we've discussed, choice is the key. We must challenge ourselves: Am I willing to invest time feeding myself with what is pure, lovely, and excellent, and turn away from things that drain me, bring me down, and make me lazy? As with physical exercise, spiritual discipline starts with a belief that it's both possible and necessary. After the belief, we must decide with resolve to do whatever it takes to change.

If we seriously want to follow Jesus as His disciple and lead others to Him, growing in our relationship with Him and allowing Him to transform us is not an option. It is a *necessity*.

Once we make the decision to move away from the world and move closer to Jesus, we need to identify the worldly areas of influence in our lives and then take steps toward spiritual fitness in those areas. The next sections address moving from "F.A.T." to "F.I.T.":

- from Feelings (lust of the flesh) to Following,
- from All-about-me (pride of life) to I AM, and

- from Taking (lust of the eyes) to Thanksgiving.

Feelings to Following: What am I Feeding?

(LUST OF THE FLESH)

"I don't feel like it."
"Because I felt like it."
"Because I no longer have any feelings for _____
(you, God, prayer)."
"He needs to understand how I feel!"
"I can't help myself!"
"If it feels good, do it."

Most advertising is specifically designed to appeal to the senses—*tastes great*, *sounds awesome*, or *you'll feel and look younger in just weeks*! Songs are filled with lyrics that glorify feelings. Movies are all about falling in and out of love and are full of choices based on how people feel in any given moment. Consequences for choices are minimized or non-existent in the media—the characters are just victims of their circumstances. Add the Christian-ese statements such as "feeling the anointing" and "feeling God's presence" to those advertising techniques and we can easily be swept away by the tide of our emotional culture.

I'm not saying that feelings in and of themselves are wrong. Jesus, as a man, was full of emotion. But His feelings never ruled his actions; His focus was fixed on doing the will of His Father who was His only guide. When we focus on our feelings, giving them too much attention or allowing *them* to be our guide, we become tossed here and there and quickly lose control. Our feelings take the throne and become our idol, and then we wonder why our lives are so unstable.

Why do we continue to let our emotions rule us? One reason is because it allows us to avoid accepting responsibility (see chapter 3). Since we're not in control, obviously what happens is not our fault—we're just innocent victims, like the characters in the movies we watch.

"Hey, it's not my fault I'm overweight—I just can't help myself when it comes to food!"

"I really want to lose weight, but I never feel like exercising."

"I'm sorry I hurt you, but you made me angry."

So how do we de-throne our feelings? Simple. Stop feeding them everything they want. Deny them. Put off the old self, and put on the new self full of righteousness and holiness. The old self includes our flesh: sin, the old ways, the corrupted nature.

> You were taught, with regard to your former way of life, to put off your old self, which is being corrupted by its deceitful desires; to be made new in the attitude of your minds; and to put on the new self, created to be like God in true righteousness and holiness.
>
> — Ephesians 4:22-24

Our flesh is kept alive and kicking when we "feed" it —when we:

Exchange the World's Ways for God's Ways 93

- give in to the temptation and the old ways and make poor choices
- keep speaking and believing the lies that we've always lived by
- refuse to allow God to rule over that place, shine His light, and reveal His truth

---

When we start to experience the death of the old fleshly self, we often panic and think, *Oh no, part of me is going to be lost forever. I must hang on!* We end up blocking God's work in our lives.

We fail to realize the basic truth that how we were in our old self is not how we really are as a child of God. The death of the old life is the only way to experience the resurrection of the new life God has already died to give us. We must choose to feed our spirits and starve our flesh, walking in obedience to God instead of going wherever our feelings lead us.

I've met so many people who sincerely believe they are powerless to control their flesh and, for example, cannot stop eating junk food. They have become victims of their flesh instead of overcomers by the power of the Holy Spirit. Not only does this rob them of true peace and joy and a whole host of other blessings, but it is also an insult to the Holy Spirit. What they've said, in essence, is that His power is not great enough. This is an open invitation for Satan, our enemy, to bring condemnation and guilt.

So yes, starving our flesh is a matter of belief as well

as a matter of choice. Whatever we believe, and therefore dwell on, has power. If we truly believe we are powerless to stop eating, we are just that. We must attack that wrong belief by investing time in knowing God's Word, and allowing it to change the way we think. Then we must obey what it says no matter how we feel. We don't ignore our feelings or suppress them, but neither do we allow them to rule our choices. Instead of doing things our way, we lay down our lives, deny ourselves, pick up our cross, and follow Jesus. We show our love for God by living His way and not ours.

> Then he said to them all: "Whoever wants to be my disciple must deny themselves and take up their cross daily and follow me.
>
> — Luke 9:23

> We know that we have come to know him if we keep his commands. Whoever says, "I know him," but does not do what he commands is a liar, and the truth is not in that person. But if anyone obeys his word, love for God is truly made complete in them. This is how we know we are in him: Whoever claims to live in him must live as Jesus did.
>
> — 1 John 2:3-6

We obey as a choice of our will, not because we have a feeling to do this or that. This is a simple concept, although it is not always easy to put into practice because in many of us, our flesh is strong.

Finally, we must stop the flow of feeling-oriented messages into our spirits by exchanging the time we spend feeding on emotionally-charged entertainment with time feeding on the spiritual food provided by the Bible, music that honors God, fellowship, and time alone with God. Every one of our choices will either lead us closer to Jesus or numb us to Him by causing barriers between Him and us. We need to resolve to protect what we watch, what we read, what we hear, and what we eat.

All-About-Me to "I AM": Who's in Charge?

(Pride of Life)

> "If you don't look out for yourself, who will?"
> "God helps those who help themselves."
> "Just believe in yourself and you can do anything you want!"
> "I'm the maker of my own destiny!"
> "My life is mine—no one has the right to tell me what I can and can't do."
> "If God didn't want me to make decisions, He wouldn't have given me a brain."
> "It's my body and I can do what I want with it."

These messages from the world are designed to keep us in control and self-sufficient, pridefully depending on ourselves for everything. The results are not peace and joy but frustration and anger at ourselves and others when we can't make things happen the way we want. This sin area isn't called the "pride of life" for nothing. Instead of reading the Bible to know Jesus and trust Him more, we can tend to read it like a "how to" manual and try to follow it in our own strength and in our own way, to get something for ourselves. We don't want to depend on God; we want a formula to follow. We say, "Okay, Lord, I'm going this way, bless me," and then complain when things don't work out and God doesn't cooperate with our plan.

We avoid asking for the Lord's help or direction because deep down inside we know He won't bless selfish motives, but then we run to Him when our way of doing things fails. We may even find ourselves stubbornly stuck in this cycle because we refuse to admit our need and then give the controls fully to the Lord.

Why are we so reluctant to trust God with everything? One reason is because the world is increasingly void of any reference or mention of God or His great love for us. When we don't know someone, and we don't know that person cares deeply for us, we find it difficult to trust that person. If we neither trust nor believe that person has our best interests at heart, what motivation do we have to obey and follow him? The same is true when it comes to how we relate to God. We don't trust Him because we don't *know* Him.

Knowledge of and trust in God's voice and His love for us is not something that happens in a one-time encounter. We get to know God's voice and learn to trust Him because of a day-by-day choice to involve God in all that we say and do. Again, we must read His Word continually to know how much He treasures and values us; and we must step out in the faith we have already attained. I am a definite work-in-progress with absorbing how much He loves me into every fiber of my being.

The stepping-out-in-faith part is an area of my life where I have failed and continue to fail in little ways and in big ways. As I mentioned several times, I am blessed (or maybe cursed) with an analytical mind. Because of this, I tend to lean on my own understanding, which hinders both my ability to hear God and my desire to stop and ask Him for direction. Many times as I've left the house I've had a random thought, *Take such-and-such with you.* Almost immediately, my own thought responded, *No, I won't need that.* Instead, I should have stopped to ask, *Lord, is that You?* Later, the need for what I didn't bring becomes apparent, along with that random thought that I dismissed. I can only admit, *Oh, that* was *You, Lord,* and then either go back to get the item, or make do without it. God was trying to make my life easier as He so delights in doing, and I missed it.

Another way we take control, and often don't even see it, is to use Bible verses to infer direction from the Lord that He is not providing. Yes, even the Bible can become a substitute for the Lord when it's not His direction that takes us there, or when we are reading out of context or with the wrong intent.

Many years ago I dated a man whom I thought the Lord brought into my life to marry because I had felt "led" to read verses about marriage and children and from that inferred that he was "the one." But all the Lord had directly told me was to "love him, accept him, and speak the truth to him." Instead of seeking godly counsel for confirmation (sometimes God speaks through others more clearly than we can hear on our own, especially concerning matters of the heart), I decided to avoid my friends altogether. I kept dating this man. As a result, we were both hurt when things didn't work out between us. In fact, God had to move me 700 miles away to another state to completely end the relationship.

I've also had some success stories. I wanted to buy a Bible for a friend, and I kept being drawn to a King James Version translation. Since I find that version hard to read, I couldn't see how the Lord could possibly want me to get that one for my friend. But, I also couldn't argue with the peace I had when I picked up that particular Bible. So I bought it and gave it to my friend. She loved it and told me how she thought the "language was just so beautiful."

Another time was when my husband Don first became a disciple of Jesus. He wanted some music, so I compiled a music cassette for him. (If you don't know what a cassette is, ask someone who was born before 1980.) He and I both liked rock style music, but the only songs I had peace about including on the cassette were soft, slow-tempo worship songs. So I made the cassette with the slow songs and gave it to him. He talked for months about how the music helped him experience God's nearness and how God spoke to him each time he played it.

From those examples and many others, I've learned that one of the most certain indicators that we are not walking in God's will and didn't seek His guidance is when we don't have His peace—the peace that passes all understanding.

> Do not be anxious about anything, but in every situation, by prayer and petition, with thanksgiving, present your requests to God. And the peace of God, which transcends all understanding, will guard your hearts and your minds in Christ Jesus.
>
> — Philippians 4:6-7

I'm not talking about a feeling, but a deep down *knowing* from the Holy Spirit that you are in complete agreement with God and with what He wants for you at that moment. You may *feel* anxious, nervous, or even a bit afraid, but deep down you know that it's what God wants you to do.

I once made plans for friends to come visit. Right before they finalized the plans, I realized I didn't have God's peace about the visit. Instead of talking to them about it, I figured that since they wanted to come, and since I wanted them to come, everything would work out. I said, "Yes, come on down!" They bought plane tickets and we made final arrangements.

The week before their visit, I found out why they were

not supposed to come. It had nothing to do with them, but with circumstances in my life that changed. God knew all that would happen and had tried to show me by lack of His peace that I would not need company when those particular dates rolled around. I didn't listen. Therefore I had another choice to make: let them come anyway, or obey the Lord and tell them not to come. Fortunately, I chose to obey, but the cost was high. Our friendship changed after that day, plus I had to pay for their unused airline tickets.

We are all in some state of transferring control over to the Lord, seeing how much better He does with our lives, and learning to fully know His voice. Very few people can become disciples of Jesus and immediately fully know God's grace and mercy, and turn everything in their lives over to Him. I'm so envious of those who learn that early. (Oops, I mean, I'm *excited* for them!) But that's the goal – to have Him be Lord over our relationships, our finances, our time, our investments, our dreams, our desires—yes, everything!

God wants control of it all because He knows He can do so much more with our lives than we can ever do on our own. He will gladly and gently lead us toward giving it all to Him, one step at a time, if only we let Him. Without Him in the driver's seat, it is impossible to live life to the fullest, and thereby walk in His love and bring the Kingdom of God to those around you.

Taking to Thanksgiving: Where is my Focus?

(Lust of the Eyes)

> "If you want it, go for it."
> "Life is short—take all you can get!"
> "Why wait when I can have it now?"
> "Go for the gusto!"
> "How come *they* can do it and I can't?"
> "You deserve _____ (that job, vacation, new TV) —why not?"
> "They're no better than you and *they* have one!"

All of these messages are designed to get us to act on impulse and emotion to gain something for ourselves. This often leads us to live way beyond our means and make hasty decisions we regret later when the bill arrives. We whip out our credit cards and act quickly before we lose that great deal. We reason that whatever *it* is, we are meant to have it because we work hard and deserve to have the best. And we want it *now*.

Waiting on the Lord is sometimes painful, and we don't always get things our way. Again, we reason and rationalize, *What difference does it make if I do it now or wait to see if the Lord says I can have it?*

We also tend to want what others have from a sense of competition. Or to define ourselves by what we own. Instead of being thankful for what we have and where we are, we constantly compare our status to others and then we're motivated to act so that we measure up. We confuse abundant life and blessings with possessions. We see it, we want it; after all, we deserve it. Our focus is on what we see and how we can get it for ourselves. Sometimes even when we get what we want, we're still not satisfied.

One morning, the Lord drew my attention to Ecclesiastes 6:2:

> God gives some people wealth, possessions and honor, so that they lack nothing their hearts desire, but God does not grant them the ability to enjoy them, and strangers enjoy them instead. This is meaningless, a grievous evil.

I did not understand. God gave the man riches, and then God didn't allow him to enjoy them? Why not?

Maybe it's a lesson on the focus of satisfying your soul (flesh, mind, will, emotions). The man desired all of those things for his soul—he wanted to live a good life here on earth, full of earthly pleasures. But the possessions turned out to be useless because God then allowed something in the man's life—maybe health issues—that didn't enable him to enjoy what he had.

Maybe it's a lesson on desiring earthly things versus eternal things. The man died and could not take any of his prize possessions with him. Plus, all possessions can be either broken, lost, or destroyed, so setting his heart too much on earthly things and building life around his things didn't bring him peace. Maybe God took away his enjoyment in an attempt to get him to change his focus.

Exchange the World's Ways for God's Ways 103

Maybe it's a lesson on ownership. The man appears to have taken those things for his own instead of recognizing that he was just a steward—God owns it all. Instead of being thankful to God, he pridefully accumulated them as his right. He did not acknowledge that God gave him the talents and gifts he had to earn, have, and keep his possessions. While God desires to bless us with things of the world for our enjoyment, we always need to hold them loosely and be willing to give them away as He leads.

Whatever the full meaning, one thing is now clear to me: everything we are and all we have is a gift from God and is intended to be used for His purposes. He created everything, so He, therefore, has ownership rights over all. When we forget that and live as owners rather than as stewards, using what we have for our pleasures instead of His eternal purposes, God can take what we have and give it to someone else. That doesn't mean we can't enjoy life here on earth, but if we stop seeking the kingdom first with what we are given, we may find that all other things are taken away from us.

Sadly, for some people this principle applies to their relationships.

> "We love each other and are getting married anyway, so why wait to have sex?"
> "She makes me so happy—I can't live without her!"
> "I'm so tired of being alone and I know the Lord has said I'd have a husband. I know this person

may not be all I wanted, or maybe even the Lord's best, but he's good enough."

We settle for what we can have now and what the world tells us is "love" instead of allowing Jesus to fulfill what He has for us in His way and in His time. Our focus is not really on the other person and what's best for them, or on God and what He'd want for us, but on ourselves and how another person can make us happy, fulfill us, or provide what we need. Often God will answer our prayer, "God, I want *Your* choice for my mate," by ending a relationship we've started. We shake our fist at Him and wonder what He's doing to us instead of being thankful that He's saved us from making a mistake.

One last and very evident manifestation of our self-centeredness and take-what's-mine mentality is our entitlement-based culture. If *you* have something I need, *I* have a right to have it. Once again the focus is on *me*, what I need, and what I have a "right" to. Or if you have it, you must give it to me. Or, if I can't find the job I want, or don't really want to work, someone else will take care of me.

We miss the Lord's best by grabbing what we want now, instead of waiting on the Lord and being thankful for what He's given us. And we miss out by taking ownership instead of recognizing it's all His anyway and allowing Him to direct how we spend our money or use our possessions. The result is death to our peace, destruction to the very best life He died to give us, and a slow and steady burial under all that with which the enemy wants to bombard us.

To see where you stand with ownership, do a quick inventory of your most prized possessions, including your relationships. Ask yourself, *What if God asked me to give 'x' away*? and see how your heart reacts. If you sincerely want to seek God's kingdom first, be ready for God to move on your behalf and remove anything or anyone in your life that is in His way. And be thankful when He does just that!

Let's pray!

Dear Jesus,

Please help me obey You rather than follow my feelings. Show me what feeds my emotions in a negative way and help me exchange it for what will positively influence me.

Take the reins of my life and help me get myself out of the way. I want You to lead me, and I want to learn how to better hear Your voice. I want my life to be about You and Your glory, not me and my comfort or my way.

Thank You for all You've given me. Please help me to remain thankful in all circumstances, for the good and the bad, recognizing that Your mercy and grace are enough for whatever I need. Help me to be content and not strive for what You are not providing.

In Your name I pray, Amen.

Chapter 11
Share Your Testimonies

In my own walk as a disciple of Jesus, I've found tremendous encouragement in hearing the testimonies (personal stories) of others and how God worked in their lives. Not only from the Bible—those whose lives are shared with such brilliant color—but also of those I know and have seen gain victory over their struggles. One's testimonies are powerful because no one can challenge or take away from your own experience. Here are a few God-stories I hope will encourage and bless you. As many have told me, I now tell you: If I can have God-stories, so can you!

RIGHT TO MY FRONT DOOR

Oh Lord, I am so content being single! It's just You and me, and I don't care if we're like this forever! So if You ever want me to get married, You'll need to bring the man to my front door!

That was my prayer on my back porch on January 20, 2000, as I was basking in the moonlight and enjoying

God's presence. I had made the above statement about getting married tongue-in-cheek while talking to a friend a few months earlier, and I reiterated it in prayer to make sure the Lord had heard me.

At the time of that declaration I had been single and not dating anyone for a long time. After many years of moaning about not finding a husband, wondering what God was doing, and asking why so-and-so was getting married and I wasn't, I had finally come to a place of complete surrender and contentment with being single. At church, I was preparing to conduct a workshop titled, "The Joys of Living Single: Overcoming the Barriers to Love." Friends and family were awesome, my job was good, and I had just bought a new house. Life was wonderful. Finally, I had victory in this area and had fully embraced being thankful. I truly didn't need, or even want, a husband.

Little did I know that my life was about to radically change. Actually, the change started six months earlier when my then-future husband and I bought houses across the street from each other. Due to our different schedules and lifestyles, it was almost impossible for us to meet. Over the next several months, I would learn that when we are willing to give our desires and even our hurts to God, give up our dreams for His dreams for us, and be thankful for where we are, He truly does more than we could ever ask or think. Yes, with God all things are possible (Matthew 19:26) – even 20 inches of snow in Raleigh, North Carolina.

On January 24, just four days after my back porch declaration, Raleigh was *buried* under 20 inches of snow.

Early that morning, I heard the scrape of snow shovels coming up my front walkway. I looked out my front window to see Don and his next-door neighbor cleaning off my sidewalk. *What gentlemen*, I thought. They shoveled all the way up to my front door. Something about Don's eyes held my attention, and with all the snow keeping us somewhat homebound, we started talking. Turns out, we had much in common. Although he didn't yet know the Lord, he had many questions and I could tell the Lord was working in his heart and life.

I could also tell the Lord was breaking me down. *Okay, Lord, did You not hear me last week?* I seemed to have traded contentment and stability for the emotions of a 16-year-old with a crush. Thankfully, I had strong roots and awesome support from my family and from friends at church. And, thankfully, I had learned from past failures that I needed them. As months went by and the friendship grew between us, by the Lord's grace, I could focus on what Don needed, which was to be rooted in God and not in a dating relationship with me.

This wasn't always easy. I spent many early mornings and late nights wrestling with God over my emotions (I quickly developed feelings of love for Don) and desires (I had prayed for a mature disciple of Jesus who was strong in the Bible and a leader) and how they didn't seem to be lining up. Don was a new disciple of Jesus, one whose character and knowledge of the Word was in the infant stage. In addition, Don kept telling me I was not his type. My emotions were all over the board. I struggled daily to not let them rule.

But I thank God He is bigger than all of our shortcomings, insecurities, questions, and personal evaluations. God knew I needed a man with a heart after God like David—one who God could grow into that mighty man of God I prayed for.

Our friendship continued to blossom under God's direction. Through another series of events only God could orchestrate, we became husband and wife. But not the way I had dreamed: me in a white dress, family and friends surrounding us, big celebration afterwards. In fact, there was no planning at all. Don asked me to marry him on Sunday night, and we were married Monday morning in the church prayer room, dressed in jeans, and with only a few witnesses. Then we called our families to tell them right before leaving that afternoon on our vacation-turned-honeymoon to England and Ireland.

To this day, we've called the January 2000 snowstorm "our snow." We know the Lord brought that snow so we could meet, just like His hand guided our steps six months earlier to two houses for sale across the street from each other. I'm so thankful I didn't miss the wonderful blessing that is my marriage to Don. The cost of giving up my dreams to receive what the Lord had for me was like paying a penny for a million dollar mansion. Suffice it to say, it has been well worth it.

God had indeed brought my husband right to my front door. And He can do that for you, too.

From My Plan to God's

All my life I've had a plan. It didn't matter what the situation, my logical mind could formulate a plan for it.

And my plans weren't only for me; they were for everyone around me. I especially had plans for (and you may guess what's coming next) ...my husband!

Don and I both knew God ordained our marriage. And, with so much of our story not going according to *my* plan, it's a miracle we ever *got* married. I also knew God chose me to help Don become the man of God he was destined to be. After all, I was *so much more* of a mature follower of Christ than Don, so I believed my help was invaluable. I entered the marriage strong and confident in the Lord. I had been cultivating my relationship with God for years and had first-hand experience with how He had transformed my life. It was *obviously* my duty and responsibility to pass along all I'd learned to Don for his benefit.

So once in the marriage, I took the attitude, *Okay, Lord, I can take it from here.*

Big mistake!

Pride deceived me into thinking that because of my maturity, I needed less time with the Lord. With all my godly background, I believed I knew what was best for both Don *and* for our marriage. I gradually but steadily slid down that slope of relying less on the Lord and more on my own experience and strength. I tried and tried and *tried* to take control over Don's spiritual growth while ignoring my own.

The sobering truth is that if my husband were not a man so strongly devoted to God, my "help" would have ended our marriage.

During the first years of our marriage, we endured (or should I say, *Don* endured) many cycles of me trying to fix him, repenting and letting him go, experiencing peace in our house, then becoming discontented and trying to fix him again. By the grace of God, and my continued choices to allow God to dig deeply into areas I didn't want to see, this fix-repent-peace-discontentment cycle was finally broken. I had to be willing to see myself for the ugly, controlling, sinful woman I was and to see how others viewed my sinful pride. I remember one time when I was praying about hurtful words someone had said to Don, without missing a beat the Lord said, *What about your words?*

My heart broke. I realized that, not only had I said hurtful words in private, but I'd also said very disrespectful words concerning him in front of others.

As I repented of my behavior I began to see God working in both of our lives. I was still reaping what I had sown through years of sin; but, thankfully, the grace of God is more powerful than my sin.

I am blessed beyond measure with God's choice for me in Don. While he may not have a formal seminary degree, God brought me a man with a heart after God, like David, and an inner strength, wisdom, and gentleness that is exactly what I need. What Don brings to my life is more than I could have ever asked or imagined. We've also had some very rough times, and both agree that only our individual relationships with the Lord kept us together through those times. Our growth together as one in marriage, and what the Lord has been able to accomplish in our lives and through us, is truly amazing!

Today I still have a plan, and that is to know and follow God's plan alone.

• • •

Killing the Flesh

I'm often asked if I drive the speed limit.

My answer to this a year ago would have been, "I usually drive nine miles per hour over the speed limit, just enough so as not to get a ticket. And when I'm following someone going faster, I will often follow their lead to keep out of ticket trouble." When driving, I was on a mission to get where I was going, and would consequently be pumped up every time I got behind the wheel.

Now, my answer is, "Yes, I drive the speed limit." I set the cruise control within a mile or two right around the posted speed limit and do my best to stay there. I don't make a legalistic, stressful effort to go exactly the speed limit, even though I could. Then I'd be so proud of myself that I'd have lots of room for boasting and that would pose another problem all its own. My goal is to respect the law and the posted speed limits. No other single change in my life has killed more of my flesh or brought me more immediate peace than making the simple change to obey the speed limit laws.

Learning to drive the speed limit started with thoughts I had about why I was driving so fast and why I wasn't obeying the speed limit. Like all of us, I rationalized my nine-over position with many forms of justification. I'm sure you've heard most of them and can add a few of your own. But the bottom line is that our reasons are just excuses to justify breaking a law that we've been told to obey. For about a month, I experienced increasing discomfort in my spirit every time I was in the car. I didn't want to acknowledge that my thoughts might be God speaking because then I'd need to listen. (And I knew He'd tell me to slow down!) So, I wrestled inside but never directly asked the Lord what He thought.

About that time, I had a haircut scheduled. Looking back, the Lord's timing was evident. He had been preparing me to hear Him whether I asked or not. I arrived at the shop early that morning so I had time to stop by and visit one of my friends who worked there. As I walked into her area, she was excitedly sharing with her customer about how the Lord had just spoken strongly to her about driving too fast. She said God told her that it was disobedient, sinful, and prideful of her to think she was above the law. If she wanted to be stronger in Him and experience all that He had for her, she needed to stop speeding around everywhere and obey that law.

Ding, ding, ding, ding, ding!

Sigh.

Okay, Lord, I get the point.

We continued to talk about some of the reasons we felt it was okay to drive fast, but it all boiled down to one basic reason: we felt like it! Who were we hurting anyway? We wanted to get where we were going and get there *now*. And it was our car so we had a right to drive it how we wanted. She shared how much it killed her flesh to drive so much slower, yet the Lord had indeed blessed her with more of Himself and an increasing knowledge of and hunger for Him.

So, I changed, but not completely. Not at first. I decided that it was okay to be within the don't-get-a-ticket range of about four miles per hour over the limit, to which my husband responded, "You're still speeding."

"But I'm within the grace allowed by the law."

He grinned and shrugged. And the Holy Spirit nudged me again. Okay, well, yes, I was still speeding. I had to repent and submit to God's way (obedience to the law) and give up my way.

It still hurts in some places where the road begs for a higher speed limit, or when everyone is speeding past me, or when someone is following on my bumper because they can't pass my car. Trips that previously took four hours now take me an extra 20 minutes. My flesh continues to die daily, and at times it goes kicking and screaming.

But the exchange of my way for God's results in an incredible amount of peace. I no longer need to constantly scan the roads to see where a police car may be. I am no longer frustrated by other drivers who don't drive like I do. My anxiety level while driving has dropped. And best of all, with each day of death to my flesh, my sense of God's nearness has increased. I hear Him more clearly, I talk to Him more regularly, and our times in the car are just plain sweet.

More than ten years later, as I work on updates to this original testimony, I realize I've slipped and need to repent all over again. God nudges me whenever I inch over the speed limit and I don't always respond. Imagine that, my own testimony convicting me years later!

Time to recommit.

Waiting ... and Waiting ... and Waiting ...

When I originally wrote this chapter, I was in my 50s and waiting for the Lord to bring me a baby I believed He promised me. I had a dream, others heard from God in their prayers that Don and I would have a son, and I believed with all my heart God would answer our own prayers and give us children. Not adopted children, but birth children. This is what I shared in the first version of this book:

> Needless to say, the seesaw of emotions as I wait for the Lord to bring me children has made for a very unusual journey, filled with lots of blessing, disappointment, excitement, discouragement, and pain. Often just when I think I'm okay with not having children, the Lord reveals my heart to me through my circumstances. Over and over again, I have watched other women with the children I didn't have. I have grieved to the point of being in so much pain I couldn't attend a friend's baby shower. Then I reach a place where I'm fine about having no children and I happily move along. Then another new birth close to home, and wham, I'm right back down again.
>
> Finally, the Lord revealed to me the source of my pain: envy! I am the oldest of four children. And, unlike the others, I had been through two marriages and divorces. At a time when I had been single for almost ten years, my three siblings were all married (all first marriages), and two of the three had children. That particular Thanksgiving, I was full of the Lord and His goodness, and finally felt content with everything going on in my life, including my singleness. I had a great church, good friends, a fruitful career, and an awesome relationship with the Lord.

Yes indeed, I was one thankful chick! In fact, I was so thankful that I was bursting at the seams to share my heart at dinner. As is our custom, each person shares something for which they are thankful. I joyfully bubbled over with how much the Lord was doing in my life and how content I was at that moment—husband or not.

Then I discovered that my bubble of joy was amazingly and surprisingly fragile. It burst right then and there with just a few simple words uttered calmly by my brother-in-law, Tim.

"I'm thankful," he said, "that my wife is going to have a baby next year." As everyone took in what he meant, tears flowed around the table. Wow, the baby of the family was having a baby! I couldn't believe it.

The rest of the dinner was a blur. In fact, the rest of the weekend was a depressing, angry haze. I managed to paste on a smile and shed some tears, but inside I was seething, *How could You do this to me, God? Now everyone else in my family is not only married, but they will also all have children, except me. Some God You are!*

My mom, bless her heart, tried to help by acknowledging that it must be hard for me to hear this. That helped a little, but the facts are the facts, and the only One who could have made it better remained silent.

As I drove home, I lamented to the Lord. *You just have no idea how much this hurts,* (as if He didn't know). He responded gently, but firmly: *It's not hurt, it's envy, and you need to take it to the Cross.*

Talk about the proverbial cold water in the face. My

tears instantly dried, and I knew in my heart He spoke exactly the truth that I needed to hear.

Without delay, I repented and chose to bless my sister. Just as immediately as He spoke, the bitterness, hurt, and anger vanished. In their place my heart was filled with love for her and excitement about her news. The whole exchange of my ways for God's took less than five minutes.

I'd like to say this was the end of my envy of women with children, but only recently have I truly been able to say, like Paul, that I am content with or without. Yes I have victory now, but remember that it took over 15 years for me to come to this point. If you are also struggling with an issue such as this, don't be hard on yourself when the victory takes time. Just keep facing God, be willing to call sin what it is, repent, and keep pressing forward.

We are in our 60s now, ten years later. It's final: God's answer to our prayers for children is "no." After a season of wrestling with "why?" we realized there's no answer to that question this side of heaven (and in heaven we most likely won't care). We learned to stop second-guessing ourselves with questions like "What did we do or not do?" and "Did God think we'd be bad parents?" We also learned through this and many other examples in our lives that we hear imperfectly and people get words imperfectly (1 Corinthians 13:9). Sometimes we want something so much, and others want it for us, that we misread "signs" along the way.

We still feel sad on Mother's Day and Father's Day,

but that momentary human sadness doesn't come *close* to how joyful and thankful we are for the life God has given us. To be honest, I am glad God said "no." I would not be the person I am today if my life was any other way.

Obey and the Feelings will Follow

I remember Charles Stanley saying in one of his teachings, "Obey and the feelings will follow." I have been blessed to experience this very dramatically, not once, but twice.

The first time, I was "righteously" angry with friends who had really put me out. In 1996, Hurricane Fran ripped through Raleigh on a Friday and left a wide path of destruction in its wake. My friends usually hosted a Sunday evening Bible study, and when we showed up at their house the Sunday after the storm, no one was home. They had been at church that morning and hadn't said anything about cancelling. They could have at least had the common courtesy to call us later when their plans changed. We drove all the way out there, a whole 15-minute drive, for nothing.

The following Sunday at church, I overheard that they had no power and had gone to stay with family close by. They'd had no way to get in touch with anyone because it was such short notice. Furthermore, they and their children had been forced to stay with family for nearly a week until their power had been restored.

Even after hearing that, I still felt hurt and angry. A little voice inside said, *Ask her how she's doing*.

What? Me? Ask her? She hasn't apologized for not being there, nor has she come to me, so why should I go to her?

But I knew it was the Lord's voice. So even though I still felt angry, I chose to do as He said. After church, I went to their car, leaned in, and said to her, "How are you doing?" Immediately after the words left my mouth, I felt compassion and love for her and felt for what it must have been like to have to pack up your kids, leave your house, and live out of suitcases for almost a week. I was so stunned I missed her answer, but have remembered the impact of that moment to this day.

Years later, my husband Don and I were on the way home from a long trip. I was driving and Don was sleeping. He woke up as I started to get tired and needed a restroom break. I thought, *Good. As soon as I can stop, he can drive and I can sleep.* I didn't try to talk to him yet because he likes time to wake up quietly.

Then his friend called. They talked and talked and talked, right through a stop at the rest area and continued on after he started to drive. I was tired and cranky and all I wanted to do was get some sleep. I laid the seat back and tried to doze off, but the intermittent talking made sleep impossible. After I had driven such a long way and let him sleep and tried to do what he wanted by giving him time to wake up, my flesh was roaring for some justice. *Couldn't he see that I was trying to sleep?*

I had two choices: 1) I could speak out of my flesh with some sarcastic remark and sour face; or 2) I could simply ask nicely if he'd be done with his conversation soon because I wanted to sleep. By some miracle, I chose the second option. As soon as the words left my mouth, the irritation left my emotions. The change happened so quickly that it startled me. I was no longer angry and actually felt love for Don. He ended his conversation and I laid the seat back to sleep, still amazed at the instant transformation of my emotions.

What these two events taught me yet again is that when we choose to say or do what is right, God's grace is right there to kill the flesh and energize the spirit. Will there always be an emotional change? No. But the only way there can or will be a change is to choose to live by the Spirit and not be guided by our emotions.

THE LITTER INCIDENT

One morning after church, my husband and I ventured out to a local paved greenway trail for a bike ride. The sun was hot, the sky blue, the breeze cool, the trail in excellent condition, with a symphony of natural sounds all around, and only a few folks out and about. We were enjoying everything about the ride.

Until I spotted it: an empty coffee cup on the side of the trail.

Can you believe it? I thought, with the appropriately condemning shake of my head, *Some people are just so stup--*

They didn't know they dropped it.

Abruptly, the Lord interrupted me. And as only He can do, He graciously revealed to my heart that I was judging again.

Ouch – seriously Lord? I judged them?
Silence.

Okay, so someone was careless and not paying attention, and lost their cup... which means, yes, they littered. Intentional or not, didn't I have a valid point about litter not being right? Yes. But did I have the right to label them as Head of the Greenway Trail Littering Brigade?

The same is true for many people who do things that hurt or annoy us: they didn't know. In fact, often times they have no idea that we are hurt or offended, and their action wasn't about us at all. Instead of trying to see from their viewpoint, we often jump to self-centered, snap judgments. All of a sudden, they are Card Carrying Members of the "Against Us" club, guilty until proven innocent to our satisfaction.

Okay, so I understand I need to forgive this person who unintentionally littered. No problem, they'll probably be upset when they realize it. But wait, I also need to forgive them if they intentionally marred the pristine landscape with their trashy and dirty used cup?

Silence.

And what about people who hurt us, Lord, what about them? I understand forgiving someone who makes a mistake, but what if their primary intention was to hurt us? What if they even meant to destroy us? I need to forgive them too?

By this time, I realized my "conversation" with God was actually a monologue. Then I remembered something Jesus said on the Cross: "Father, forgive them. They didn't know what they were doing" (my paraphrase of Luke 23:34).

Wait, how could those people not know they were killing Jesus? I mean, after all, isn't death the main intent of a crucifixion? Yet Jesus said, "They didn't know what they were doing."

Maybe it's because He perfectly knew and understood everything about them. He knew their motives were influenced by their weaknesses, their fears, and their failures. Perhaps He knew that in all of their human-ness, there was no way for them to fully "know" what they were doing.

Likewise, He knows you and me, completely and fully, in a way we can't even begin to comprehend. And knowing us, He forgives us too—even when we know better than to throw out that litter.

> For God did not send his Son into the world to condemn the world, but to save the world through him.
>
> — John 3:17

So whether another's sin (or littering) is intentional or not, we are called to forgive. We have no right to rush to a snap judgment.

Next time I am tempted to jump to conclusions, I hope I remember the Litter Incident.

GOD KNOWS OUR HEARTS...AND HEALS THEM

The Lord showed me my heart one day. And it was ugly.

When I arrived at work, I spoke to a co-worker whom I'll call Joan, on the way in from the parking lot. She hardly paused long enough to listen, then answered over her shoulder as she continued to walk by.

Not to be discouraged, I went to her desk a few minutes later to continue the conversation. I thought maybe she needed to get inside quickly for some reason and that's why she didn't stop to chat. I discovered from her continued brief responses that, no, she just didn't want to talk to me.

Crushed and heart-broken, I went back to my desk. I've seen Joan enjoy friendly conversations with others about non-work topics. Since I work somewhat closely with her, I've been trying on and off for a while to join in and be friendly too. Her short answers have always bothered me a little, but until today I always managed to shrug them off. But I guess it finally hit me: *Joan just doesn't like me.*

Close to tears, I sat at my desk and talked to the Lord about why it hurt so much this time. I knew I was overreacting because I knew *I* had people I didn't especially like, and I knew it was not realistic to expect everyone to like me.

Yet my heart just hurt so much.

You know how you are with people you don't particularly like? This is how they feel when you treat them like Joan treated you.

Stunned by His truth, my heart broke even more. Oh my, yes, I've treated others just like this. Oh my, I had no idea! I didn't want to admit it, but I had to face the ugly truth that I was just like Joan. When someone I didn't like tried to talk to me and I was not interested, I gave the one-word answers and hurried to get away. And I've always felt bad about it later...but not bad enough to change.

Until now.

Oh Lord, I am so sorry.

In 2 Corinthians 7:10, Paul wrote about repentance:

> Godly sorrow brings repentance that leads to salvation and leaves no regret, but worldly sorrow brings death.

Until now, I had experienced worldly sorrow that brought death. I felt sorry for a moment after I mistreated someone, then quickly moved on, leaving a trail of hurt in my wake. But now I experienced godly sorrow that brought me to true repentance and transformed my heart. I had no doubt that the Lord had to break my heart to heal it.

In His great mercy, He gave me an immediate opportunity to reveal what He had done and to allow me to experience the joy of my changed heart.

I had a meeting scheduled with a person I had previously shunned. With my new revelation, I waited with excitement for the meeting time so I could welcome him and be friendly to him. My *like* of this person was now genuine and from my heart—my God-changed heart. The difference was nothing short of miraculous.

Once again, I am humbled and amazed at how little it takes from me—just a willing heart and a choice to obey—to receive so much from Him. I cannot change my own heart by *doing* as I can improve my physical fitness through eating right and exercise. To become more spiritually fit, my *doing* is simply to respond obediently when He initiates—He does the inside changing. I rest in Him, He works in me.

Oh, the glorious life of walking with Jesus!

That day at work the Lord showed me my ugly heart. I'm so glad He did!

Close Enough

Close enough is okay when you're describing an event but miss a few details.

Close enough is okay when you're parallel parking.

Close enough is even okay when you're hanging a picture and you're not quite at the center of the wall.

But close enough is not okay when it comes to obeying God.

One night I put the finishing touches on my submission for a book contest. As I read my entry for the last time, I paused at the line, "written in short chapters for people who don't like to read." Wow, really? Writing a book for people who don't like to read? They'll think that's crazy. I know it was the Lord who told me to write books for people who don't like to read...but they don't need to know that.

What about, "written in short chapters for people who don't have much time to read?" That made much more sense, and it's a more acceptable reason. And it's close enough to what the Lord told me. Change made, I sent it in.

The first thing on my mind when I woke up the next morning was to change that sentence. Immediately following that thought, a question: *But so what, Lord? It's such a small change, isn't it close enough? Do they really care, one way or another?*

They may not care, but I do. It's not what I told you to say.

Yes, it's a small thing. And yes, it probably didn't matter to the quality of the overall entry. But since it was directly disobedient to what God told me, I had to correct it. Partial obedience is disobedience. I changed my wording back to the original, and sent in my revised entry.

And God wasn't done with me yet.

I talked to a friend of mine on the way into work that same morning. As I pulled into my parking space at 7:55, I let her know I was at work and had to go. She was talking about an incident with her neighbor, and sharing prayer needs. I really wanted to get into work because I had a busy day, but she was still going into the details of her story.

After a few minutes, I finally cut her off with, "I'm sorry, but I've really got to run because I have a meeting at 8 o'clock." So we quickly said good-bye and I went into work.

Only one small problem: I didn't have a meeting at 8 o'clock. Well, I had work to do and had scheduled that time for a particular task. Wasn't that close enough?

No, I lied. Whatever the reason and whatever the motive, a lie is a lie. Even after a fresh lesson on obeying in the small things, I quickly and easily blurted out a lie to make myself sound more acceptable. Again. How quickly I fell.

But God! He's always there with forgiveness, correction, and courage to do the right thing...if only we are willing to reject the idea of being *close enough* and just obey Him.

I texted my friend, explained that I didn't really have a meeting but just wanted to get into work, and asked for her forgiveness. She understood. She forgave me. Yes, she's a good friend, and I'm thankful for her.

And I'm thankful for my Father who cares enough about me to teach me and correct me in the little things...and that I'm close enough to hear His voice when He does.

Dear Jesus,

Please help me to boldly share what You are doing in my life so I may encourage others. Thank You for all who encourage me by their words and their lives. Thank You for the testimonies yet to come.

In Your mighty name I pray, Amen.

Why We Are Here

No matter where you are in your journey, I hope you're encouraged to pursue a deepening relationship with Jesus. This is a prayer Paul prayed for the Ephesians from Ephesians 1:17-19 (revised here to be a personal prayer you can pray to God):

> I keep asking You, the God of our Lord Jesus Christ, the glorious Father, to give me the Spirit of wisdom and revelation, so that I may know You better.
> I pray that the eyes of my heart may be enlightened in order that I may know the hope to which You have called me, the riches of Your glorious inheritance in all Your holy people, and Your incomparably great power for all of us who believe.

I promise you this is a prayer God will answer, over time, in ways personalized just for you. He is so amazing!

You can also pray as Jesus taught His disciples in Matthew 6:9-13:

> "This, then, is how you should pray:
> 'Our Father in heaven,
> hallowed be your name,
> your kingdom come,
> your will be done,
>   on earth as it is in heaven.
> Give us today our daily bread.
> And forgive us our debts,
>   as we also have forgiven our debtors.
> And lead us not into temptation,
>   but deliver us from the evil one.'

As Jesus said to His disciples in Luke 9:23-25, the goal (why we are here) is to give up your very life *every day* to receive His life in exchange. Full surrender.

> Then he said to them all: "Whoever wants to be my disciple must deny themselves and take up their cross daily and follow me. For whoever wants to save their life will lose it, but whoever loses their life for me will save it. What good is it for someone to gain the whole world, and yet lose or forfeit their very self?

If you're still not sure if you're "right with God," so to speak, please read Chapter 2 again about becoming a disciple of Jesus. You may have never prayed, or maybe you prayed long ago but you've wandered away from your faith. Either way, now is your time to start fresh—His mercies are new every morning.

> It is because of the Lord's mercy and loving-kindness that we are not consumed, because His [tender] compassions fail not. They are new every morning; great and abundant is Your stability and faithfulness.
>
> — Lamentations 3:22-23 (AMPC)

When you are ready, pray with all your heart for God to forgive your sins, accept what Jesus did on the Cross for you, and ask for and receive new life in the Holy Spirit.

Not sure how to pray? Here is a simple prayer:

Dear Lord Jesus, I know that I am a sinner, and I ask for Your forgiveness. I believe You died for my sins and rose from the dead. I turn from my sins and invite You to come into my heart and life. I choose to trust and follow You as my Lord and Savior, starting right now.

God loves you, and He desires for you to live abundantly here on earth, with purpose and conviction, AND with Him forever in Heaven after you leave this earth. He longs to wrap His arms around you, speak encouragement to you, and transform you into the beautiful person He had in His thoughts from before you were even in the womb!

> For you created my inmost being;
> you knit me together in my mother's womb.
> I praise you because I am fearfully and wonderfully made; your works are wonderful, I know that full well.
> My frame was not hidden from you when I was made in the secret place, when I was woven together in the depths of the earth. Your eyes saw my unformed body; all the days ordained for me were written in your book before one of them came to be.

> How precious to me are your thoughts, God! How
> vast is the sum of them! Were I to count them,
> they would outnumber the grains of sand—
> when I awake, I am still with you.
>
> — Psalm 139:13-18

As you get to know the Savior more every day, a God who loves you like no other person ever could, I pray He fills the emptiness inside to overflowing with His love, peace, and joy.

He is faithful, He is able, and He is willing…if you are willing.

If you prayed to begin your relationship with Jesus, or prayed to recommit your life to Him, or if you have questions about anything you read, I'd love to hear from you. Please email me at LifeIsNotAFormula (at) gmail.com.

May the Lord bless your journey!

Endnotes

7. Repent From Your Sins

1. https://www.dictionary.com/browse/repent
2. https://www.ccel.org/e/easton/ebd/ebd/T0003100.html#T0003105

9. Grow in Intimacy with God

1. Oswald Chambers, *My Utmost for His Highest, Updated Edition* (Grand Rapids, MI: Discovery House, 1995)
2. C. S. Lewis, *A Year with C. S. Lewis, Daily Readings from His Classic Works* (New York, NY: HarperCollins, 2003)
3. Chris Tiegreen, *The One Year worship the King Devotional* (Carol Stream, IL: Tyndale House Publishers, Inc, 2008)

Made in the USA
Coppell, TX
02 December 2022